# MOBILIZING THE WILL TO INTERVENE

*18 Jan. 2010*

*For Helen Fein,*
*My favorite deli partner...*
*and scholar! / Fondly,*
*Frank*

# Mobilizing the Will to Intervene

## Leadership to Prevent Mass Atrocities

FRANK CHALK, ROMÉO DALLAIRE,
KYLE MATTHEWS, CARLA BARQUEIRO,
AND SIMON DOYLE

Published for
The Montreal Institute for Genocide and Human Rights Studies
at Concordia University
by
McGill-Queen's University Press
Montreal & Kingston · London · Ithaca

ISBN 978-0-7735-3803-0 (cloth)
ISBN 978-0-7735-3804-7 (paper)

Legal deposit third quarter 2010
Bibliothèque nationale du Québec

Printed in Canada on acid-free paper that is 100% ancient forest
free (100% post-consumer recycled), processed chlorine free

McGill-Queen's University Press acknowledges the support of the
Canada Council for the Arts for our publishing program. We also
acknowledge the financial support of the Government of Canada
through the Canada Book Fund for our publishing activities.

Library and Archives Canada Cataloguing in Publication Data

Mobilizing the will to intervene : leadership to prevent mass
atrocities / Frank Chalk ... [et al.].

Includes bibliographical references.
ISBN 978-0-7735-3803-0 (bound). –
ISBN 978-0-7735-3804-7 (pbk.)

1. Genocide intervention – Political aspects – Canada. 2. Genocide
intervention – Political aspects – United States. 3. Genocide –
Rwanda – Case studies. 4. Genocide – Kosovo (Republic) – Case
studies. 5. Genocide – Political aspects. 1. Chalk, Frank, 1937–
II. Montreal Institute for Genocide and Human Rights Studies

JZ6369.M62 2010      341.5'84      C2010-903447-3

Typeset by Jay Tee Graphics Ltd. in 10/13 Sabon

This book is dedicated to the memory of the late
Alison Des Forges, who worked tirelessly to prevent
genocide, advance accountability, and end impunity. We also
pay tribute to all the victims of mass atrocities whose lives
ended prematurely while the world stood by.

# Contents

# Abbreviations and Acronyms

APC       Atrocities Prevention Committee
CBC       Canadian Broadcasting Corporation
CIA       Central Intelligence Agency
CIDA      Canadian International Development Agency
DFAIT     Department of Foreign Affairs and International
          Trade Canada
DND       Department of National Defence
DOD       Department of Defense
DPKO      Department of Peacekeeping Operations
DRC       Democratic Republic of the Congo
FSO       Foreign Service Officer
G8        Group of Eight
HIV/AIDS  Human Immunodeficiency Virus/Acquired
          Immunodeficiency Syndrome
ICHRDD    International Centre for Human Rights and
          Democratic Development
ICISS     International Commission on Intervention and State
          Sovereignty
IPC       Interagency Policy Committee
KLA       Kosovo Liberation Army
MONUC     The United Nations Organization Mission in the
          Democratic Republic of the Congo
MP        Member of Parliament
NATO      North Atlantic Treaty Organization
NGO       Non-Governmental Organization

NSC       National Security Council
OAS       Organization of American States
OSCE      Organization for Security and Co-operation in
          Europe
PCO       Privy Council Office
PDD       Presidential Decision Directive
PMO       Prime Minister's Office
PRD       Presidential Review Decision
RPF       Rwandan Patriotic Front
R2P       Responsibility to Protect
RTLM      Radio Télévision Libre des Milles Collines
STAND     Students Taking Action Now: Darfur
START     Stabilization and Reconstruction Task Force
UN        United Nations
UNAMIR    United Nations Assistance Mission for Rwanda
UNDPKO    United Nations Department of Peacekeeping
          Operations
UNOSOM    United Nations Operations in Somalia
UNSC      United Nations Security Council
US        United States
USAID     United States Agency for International Development
USG       United States Government
W2I       Will to Intervene

# Foreword

It is no accident that Canadian General Roméo Dallaire, the commander of the UN military forces in Rwanda during the 1994 genocide, volunteered to co-direct the Will to Intervene (W2I) Project, or that his partner in formulating the study was Frank Chalk, the director of the Montreal Institute for Genocide and Human Rights Studies (MIGS) at Concordia University and a long-time history professor who lost many relatives during the Holocaust.

For those of us who work on the responsibility to protect civilians from mass atrocity crimes – and I proudly count myself in their number after having been the research director for the International Commission on Intervention and State Sovereignty (ICISS) – the tragic absence of political will to stop perpetrators of genocide, crimes against humanity, ethnic cleansing, and war crimes is an old story. It is often lamented but too rarely confronted. Standing at the very heart of this tragedy is the story of General Dallaire, denied the troop reinforcements and the freedom to act that he requested to stop the Rwandan Genocide of 1994.

Thoughtfully and constructively, *Mobilizing the Will to Intervene: Leadership to Prevent Mass Atrocities* seeks to break the cycle of indifference and confront the political will *not* to intervene that was so painfully evident in 1994. Drawing on incisive case studies contrasting American and Canadian government responses to the Rwandan Genocide and events in Kosovo in

1999, the W21 research team draws on lessons learned from its interviews with over eighty policy makers and other participants. Those still smarting from the crucial governmental decisions about Rwanda and Kosovo propose practical steps to raise the capacities of Washington and Ottawa to prevent future mass atrocity crimes.

The Will to Intervene research team builds also on important insights highlighted in two earlier reports: *The Responsibility to Protect*, issued in December 2001 by ICISS, and *Preventing Genocide: A Blueprint for U.S. Policy Makers*, released in December 2008 by the Genocide Prevention Task Force co-chaired by former US secretary of state Madeleine Albright and former secretary of defense William Cohen. *The Responsibility to Protect* laid out rigorous criteria specifying trip wires and boundaries for the actions needed at the international level, while recognizing how poorly understood the process of building the political will at home and internationally to prevent mass atrocities actually was. *Preventing Genocide* also focused on the international dimension and the threat to US national interests of failed and failing states, while decrying the corrosive effect that continued apathy to such atrocities would have on American values.

I am struck that the Will to Intervene team proposes nothing less than a paradigm shift in prevention thinking and by the reasons it gives to justify that shift. It calls on the leaders of the United States and Canada to recognize that preventing mass atrocity crimes is not just a moral duty but also a vital national interest. It points to the higher probability resulting from neglecting mass atrocities that pandemics and other epidemic diseases will breach public health defenses, that terrorism coordinated from sanctuaries in failed and failing states will penetrate our security barriers, and that lawless warlords and pirates will narrow our access to strategic raw materials, thereby undermining our competitiveness and commercial prosperity.

The W21 team urges political leaders in the United States and Canada to develop government's "soft" and "hard" power capacities to nip mass atrocities in the bud. In a globalized world criss-crossed annually by more than eighteen million commercial air flights, they correctly argue that humanitarian values,

national interests, and domestic security are inextricably inter-
twined. This reality – not just some pious plea from scholars
and activists – requires political leaders to move improved early
warning systems, innovative coordinating mechanisms, and
sophisticated response capacities to the top of the agenda.

While much of the energy devoted to implementing the recommendations of *The Responsibility to Protect* remains focused
on progress at the international level, the W21 team is mounting
local civic dialogues with leaders of business, the media, non-
governmental organizations, and governments across the United
States and Canada. They thus are encouraging every level of
government – ranging from municipal councillors and state and
provincial legislators to members of the US Congress and the
Canadian Parliament – to endorse W21's recommendations. Let
us hope that these innovative sessions guarantee W21 a sustained
and prominent place on the public's radar screen.

How fitting it would be if the rejection of General Roméo
Dallaire's brave effort to mobilize the will to intervene to halt
the Rwandan Genocide ultimately brought the United States and
Canada to stand among the leaders of an international coalition
of states willing to raise their capacities and to exercise their
wills to prevent mass atrocity crimes. More than poetic justice,
that is the real promise of *Mobilizing the Will to Intervene*.

Thomas G. Weiss
Presidential Professor of Political Science
Director of the Ralph Bunche Institute for International Studies
The Graduate Center of The City University of New York

# Preface

In 1946, the General Assembly of the United Nations passed the following resolution: "Genocide is a denial of the right of existence of entire human groups, as homicide is the denial of the right to live of individual human beings; such denial of the right of existence shocks the conscience of mankind, results in great losses to humanity in the form of cultural and other contributions represented by these human groups, and is contrary to moral law and to the spirit and aims of the United Nations. Many instances of such crimes of genocide have occurred when racial, religious, political and other groups have been destroyed, entirely or in part. The punishment of the crime of genocide is a matter of international concern.

*"The General Assembly, therefore, Affirms* that genocide is a crime under international law which the civilized world condemns, and for the commission of which principals and accomplices – whether private individuals, public officials or statesmen, and whether the crime is committed on religious, racial, political or any other grounds – are punishable."

A decade into the twenty-first century, the world is still struggling to implement these noble principles and curtail mass atrocities, which shock the conscience of humankind. Why is our record of preventing genocide and mass atrocities so poor? Since 1946, why have we done so little to halt the systematic killings of innocent civilians in Indonesia, Burundi, East Pakistan, Cambodia, East Timor, Rwanda, Sudan, and the Democratic Republic of the Congo? What stops the richest and most powerful nations on earth from vigorously combating the economic and social conditions that breed genocides? What discourages them from using their influence to interdict genocides once they are underway?

One of us, Lt. Gen. (Ret.) Roméo Dallaire, commanded the UN Assistance Mission for Rwanda during the genocide that ripped through the African country like a scythe from April to July 1994. The world sat on its hands as hundreds of thousands of Tutsis were slaughtered and any Hutu who stepped forward to offer them sanctuary was literally chopped to bits. The Security Council withdrew UN peacekeepers instead of reinforcing them. The other one of us, Professor Frank Chalk, comes from a family whose European branches were decimated in the Holocaust and, since 1978, has devoted much of his academic life to seeking answers to the questions posed above.

Believing that cutting-edge scholarly research, concrete policy proposals, and responsible activism can transform our world and make it a safer place for all, in September 2007 the Montreal Institute for Genocide and Human Rights Studies (MIGS) launched the Will to Intervene (W21) Project, a crucial initiative that focuses on the prevention of genocide and other mass atrocity crimes through the mobilization of domestic political will. This ongoing project's first phase, from 2007 to 2009, focused on producing and disseminating a detailed report – which forms the basis of the present book – identifying strategic and practical steps to raise the capacity of governments in the United States and Canada to prevent mass atrocities. To that end, the W21 Project interviewed more than eighty foreign policy practitioners and opinion shapers in the United States and Canada. Many of the interviewees participated directly in American and Canadian government decision making during the 1994 Rwandan Genocide and the 1999 Kosovo crisis. These two cases fostered much debate and discussion in the 1990s over the legitimacy of humanitarian intervention. In Rwanda, more than 800,000 innocent civilians were slaughtered over a four-month period in 1994, while the international community looked on passively and individual states evaded their responsibility to act swiftly and decisively in the face of genocide. In Kosovo, the opposite occurred. Fearing genocide in the Balkans just four years after the massacre in Srebrenica, Bosnia, a coalition of concerned countries in 1999 mounted an early response to prevent mass atrocities, channelled through the North Atlantic Treaty Organization (NATO) and under US leadership, without seeking UN Security Council authorization.

The W21 interviews furnished us with an inside view of the decision-making processes that shaped each country's response to Rwanda and Kosovo, exemplifying both a strong will to act and a failure to act. The W21 Project's researchers also wanted to understand what civil society groups and the news media could have done to ramp up the pressure on President Clinton and Prime Minister Chrétien to save lives in Rwanda. We wanted to learn if civil society played a role in the decisions of the United States and Canada to preserve lives in Kosovo and what considerations propelled the decision to intervene. We designed our questions with an eye to the future, hunting for "lessons learned," informed not only by our interviews but also by scholarly studies of US and Canadian government policies.

In studying these and other cases, the W21 researchers were struck not by the absence of the will to intervene to prevent genocide but by the presence of the will *not* to intervene, a negative thrust evident among the leaders of the United States, Canada, and other democracies when confronting the great mass atrocities of the twentieth and twenty-first centuries. These mass atrocities were surely "contrary to moral law and the spirit and aims of the United Nations," as the UN expressed it in 1946, but "moral law" and "the spirit and aims of the United Nations" carry very little weight in the national interest and partisan political calculations that shape foreign policies in the capitals of the great democracies.

The fundamental goal of this book is to identify strategic and practical steps to raise the capacity of government officials, legislators, civil servants, non-governmental organizations (NGOs), advocacy groups, journalists, and media owners and managers – in the United States and Canada – to build the political will to prevent mass atrocities. The premise of the entire W21 Project is that democratic states can and must play a leadership role in the prevention of mass atrocities. In the first phase of the W21 Project we sought to analyze how the United States and Canada – prosperous democracies sustaining robust civil societies and free media – could play leadership roles in preventing future genocides. We chose the United States and Canada as the first countries for study because without US logistical and political support very little ever gets done, while Canada possesses many years of experience in peacekeeping and has participated in most of the missions authorised by the UN Security Council. As well, the United States and Canada are key members of important intergovernmental organizations such as NATO, the Organization for Security and Co-operation in Europe (OSCE), the Group of 8, and the Organization of American States (OAS), to name just a few. Vulnerable to the consequences of mass atrocities committed overseas, the United States and Canada share common security and economic interests.

One of the major outcomes of the W21 study is the finding that when leadership at the top is absent, civil society in the United States and Canada must strongly pressure governments to broaden their concept of "national interests." Saving the lives of innocent civilians in future Rwandas and Kosovos is vital to saving lives in the United States and Canada, since more and more our security is threatened by neglected crises in faraway places. Thanks to the growth in international travel by business people, tourists, and aid workers, infectious disease outbreaks arising in once-ignored areas like the Democratic Republic of the Congo, Sudan, and Zimbabwe now pose real challenges to our public health. As well, mass atrocities undermine the foundations of political stability in entire regions of the globalized international economy and threaten our economic prosperity. Our stake in international security has converged with our stake in humanitarian principles as never before. We need to redefine our national interests more broadly, not only to help broken and failing states but also to help and protect ourselves.

W21's message to American and Canadian politicians is that to be responsible leaders they must spearhead policies and programs that prevent mass atrocities. Without leadership from the highest level of government, our countries will make little progress toward solving the recurring global problems of mass atrocities or stopping their lethal ripple effects. We lay out missed policy options that the United States and Canada could have pursued in Rwanda in 1994 and describe successful responses to early warnings in Kosovo in 1999. By providing detailed case studies of US and Canadian decision making over Rwanda and Kosovo, W21 aims to help decision makers envisage innovative and timely solutions in the future.

*Mobilizing the Will to Intervene: Leadership to Prevent Mass Atrocities* is important reading for politicians, diplomats, development practitioners, business leaders, journalists, military officials, academics, NGO representatives, and concerned citizens throughout North America. This book also contains much information that will be of interest to students of international relations, political science, security studies, journalism, and American and Canadian history. Part One of the book describes the impacts of genocide and mass atrocities, highlighting the enormous security, financial, and political costs of inaction. This section also analyzes the emerging drivers of deadly violence in the twenty-first century. Part Two contains two historical case studies analyzing how, when, and why key decisions were made by the American and Canadian governments concerning the 1994 Rwandan Genocide and the 1999 Kosovo crisis. Part Three presents our policy recommendations for our governments and explains how to generate the domestic political will that can convince them to intervene in situations where human rights violations risk spiralling into genocide.

We use the term "humanitarian intervention" in its widest sense to include the broad spectrum of tools that our governments can employ to prevent mass atrocities. These include "soft" and "hard" power tools; that is, non-military and military actions. In the preventive phase of a humanitarian intervention, the governments of the United States and Canada can offer development assistance and financial aid, technical support, training, debt reduction, and mediation. When consensual preventive measures fail and more robust action is required, they can introduce the withdrawal of visas and scholarships for children from the recalcitrant political elite, economic sanctions, arms embargoes,

xx                              Preface

the enforcement of no-fly zones, and the use of military force. W21 strongly supports the view that credible military force must be visible in the wings to potentiate non-military preventive action. Consensual soft power methods can succeed, but peace spoilers only cooperate with them when they know their forces can be neutralized.

Recognizing a substantive difference between the governing structures of the United States and Canada, the government recommendations we present are crafted separately for American and Canadian governments and legislators. In the United States, the executive branch, headed by the president, is separate from the legislative branch – the Congress – which checks and balances the power of the executive. Members of Congress sometimes vote independently, ignoring the position of the executive or the leaders of their party and responding to popular opinion within their electoral districts or to their own personal convictions. Members of Congress have the ability to frustrate or force the revision of executive appropriations proposals and other legislative initiatives.

Although both the US president and the Canadian prime minister have similar executive powers – such as the ability to deploy limited military forces without approval from their respective national legislatures – the prime minister's executive power in Canada is far greater than that of the president in the United States. The prime minister typically controls a majority of votes in the House of Commons, giving the governing party the authority to pass laws and to spend at its discretion. A string of minority governments in recent years has empowered Parliament's opposition parties as the government must seek their support to pass legislation, but it is rare that Parliament can change a majority government's course on key policies. Due to the differences between the American and Canadian systems of government – and the challenges and complexities of influencing government policy – we urge advocates to develop a firm understanding of their targets within the machinery of government before they set out to influence them.

The recommendations outlined in this book were developed after consultation with a variety of experts on international and domestic security, politics, and human rights, as well as through in-depth research in US and Canadian policy studies. w21's Research Steering Committee generously provided important feedback and strategic advice at every stage of the project. The Research Steering Committee met in Montreal in May and September of 2008. In addition, the w21 researchers consulted with academic experts at two important consultation workshops in April and November of 2008. The members of the Research Steering Committee and the Academic Consultation Group are listed in the appendices.

Our recommendations were drafted by the w21 researchers in consultation with experts and the co-directors of the project and do not necessarily represent agreement or consensus among the Research Steering Committee members, Academic Consultation Group, or interviewees. The interpretations put forward and any factual errors are those of the w21 team, not the members of the Research Steering Committee or the Academic Consultation Group.

We would like to thank the generous and principled sponsors of our project – The Simons Foundation of Vancouver, James Stanford of Calgary, the family and friends of Aaron Fish of Montreal, the Tauben Family fund of Irwin and Sara Tauben, and several offices at Concordia University, especially the Office of the Vice-President for Research and Graduate Studies, the Office of Research, and the Office for Advancement. We also wish to express our thanks to the outstanding members of our Research Steering Committee and the learned members of our Academic Consultation Group. Finally, we would like to acknowledge all those who gave their time freely for interviews with our researchers about their direct experiences and insights regarding the 1994 genocide in Rwanda and the 1999 crisis in Kosovo. Their candour and confidence in our important work, and their willingness to make time in their very busy schedules, speaks volumes about their values. We thank them.

This book was born in hope – our hope that concrete factual analyses and practical recommendations can change the way our democratically elected political leaders think and act. We ask for nothing less than a paradigm shift, a change in how our leaders view the world. Specifically, we seek to persuade the leaders of the United States and Canada to adopt an understanding of the national interest that incorporates the idea that preventing geno-cide and mass atrocities serves the interests of their people and that not doing so puts the welfare of their citizens at risk. The age of the global village has dawned. Ignoring instability and conflict leading to genocides and mass atrocities today seriously threatens the health, security, and prosperity of every one of us. We can – and must – change.

LGen (Ret) Roméo Dallaire and Frank Chalk
Co-directors of the Will to Intervene Project

MOBILIZING THE WILL TO INTERVENE

# PART ONE

# More than Humanitarianism

> Political will is not something you find if you look in the
> right cupboard. It has to be laboriously crafted, case by
> case, using the resources of both insiders and outsiders,
> bottom up from civil society and through peer group pres-
> sure from those in positions of influence nationally and
> internationally.
>
> Gareth Evans, co-chair of the International Commission
> on Intervention and State Sovereignty and former foreign
> minister of Australia

## A CALL FOR LEADERSHIP AND ACTION

Generating the international political will necessary to prevent
mass atrocities remains one of the central challenges of the twenty-
first century. First, we must recognize that the United Nations and
other international institutions are made up of national governments whose primary concern is the retention of political support from their domestic constituencies. Consequently, the key to
mobilizing international support is to first garner domestic support. This was one of the central arguments of *The Responsibility
to Protect*, the 2001 report prepared by the International Commission on Intervention and State Sovereignty (ICISS). To implement the principles of the responsibility to protect (R2P) on the
world stage, it is imperative that national strategies be developed
for the generation of domestic political will.

Gareth Evans, co-chair of the ICISS, affirms that "the loudest
and most oft-repeated lamentation of them all is that there is a

'lack of political will' to do what needs to be done." The W21 Project aims to address this deficiency for the United States and Canada by presenting innovative strategies and proposing new offices within government to prevent mass atrocities. These recommendations are divided into four thematic sections devoted to the generation of domestic political will:

1 Enabling Leadership
2 Enhancing Coordination
3 Building Capacity
4 Ensuring Knowledge

W21 uses the term "mass atrocities" to refer to the four specific crimes listed by the international community in the 2005 World Summit Outcome document: genocide, crimes against humanity, ethnic cleansing, and war crimes. Although this book focuses particularly on genocide and crimes against humanity, it does not propose to organize these four crimes in a hierarchical order, nor does it seek to become embroiled in the legal and definitional trap of what separates genocide from other mass atrocities. Fundamentally, this book aims to defend the most important human right: the right not to be murdered.

Since 2003, hundreds of thousands of civilians in Darfur, western Sudan, have been murdered, with many more displaced and forced to live in camps plagued by disease and insecurity. Besides Darfur, the Democratic Republic of the Congo, Somalia, Zimbabwe, Sri Lanka, and Burma are only a few of the countries in which civilians face high risks of mass atrocities. The failure to deter these threats represents first and foremost a political failure to uphold the emerging norm of the responsibility to protect.

The ICISS, established under the leadership of the Government of Canada and supported by UN Secretary General Kofi Annan, was initiated in 2000 to foster global discussion and offer policy guidance on humanitarian intervention, following the international community's disastrous response to the Rwandan Genocide in 1994 and the tensions generated by NATO's 1999 intervention in Kosovo. The commission's report, released in 2001, advanced the notion of "sovereignty as responsibility"

– first introduced by Francis Deng and others at the Brookings Institution in 1996 – which challenged a long-standing consensus that the principle of state sovereignty was absolute, regardless of whether a state committed serious human rights abuses against its own citizens. The report argued that state sovereignty is a privilege, not a right, and that it is derived from a reciprocal relationship of respect between the state and its citizens. At the 2005 World Summit, the UN General Assembly members, including the United States and Canada, agreed that if a state is unwilling or unable to protect its own citizens against gross violations of internationally recognized human rights, the international community must assume the responsibility to protect them. Under such circumstances, the international community has a duty to launch preventive, reactive, and rebuilding measures to protect defenseless civilians being abused by their own governments. Significantly, the UN General Assembly World Summit Outcome document singled out prevention as the most important element of the responsibility to protect. R2P has subsequently become a far-reaching international security and human rights doctrine; it demonstrates the growing recognition that sovereignty is an evolving principle intrinsically linked to the security and protection of civilians.

## INCORPORATING THE PREVENTION OF MASS ATROCITIES INTO THE NATIONAL INTEREST

This book argues that the prevention of mass atrocities should be prioritized as a vital national interest by the governments of the United States and Canada. One of the most frequently voiced arguments for explaining the international failure to prevent the Rwandan Genocide derived from government assessments that deeper involvement was not in the national interest and would ultimately result in domestic political opposition and partisan criticism.

For many of today's policy makers, national interests continue to be defined by two central considerations: national security and economic interests. Traditionally, national security threats to the territorial integrity of the state and its people were exclusively viewed as emanating from other states. Similarly, state economic interests were threatened if trade relations with other states provided trading partners with greater relative gains. Since the end of the Cold War, the increasing pace of globalization has changed the nature of international and transnational interactions. Threats to national security and economic interests no longer emanate exclusively from competing states.

> When genocide is happening, when ethnic cleansing is happening somewhere around the world and we stand idly by, that diminishes us. And so I do believe that we consider it as part of our interests, our national interests, in intervening where possible.
>
> Barack Obama, speaking as a presidential candidate in 2008

Mass atrocities, with their chaos and mass loss of life, produce shock waves – seismic wrecking balls destabilizing and destroying social, economic, health, and political infrastructures – that reverberate throughout the rest of the world. This is a cardinal lesson of the Rwandan Genocide. In the coming decade, the leaders of the United States and Canada should play a vital role in redefining their countries' national interests to include the prevention of mass atrocities. This means ending both the "stove-piping" of national interest calculations and the setting of national priorities based on narrow and dated assessments that ignore the indirect consequences of mass atrocities.

An interdependent web of relationships between states, individuals, civil society groups, and multinational corporations increasingly characterizes today's globalized world. Many countries rely on far-flung electronic communication systems, digital technologies, and computerized services to enhance their prosperity. The United States and Canada maintain extensive economic and trade relations with countries all over the world; both countries are tourist and migration destinations for people from every corner of the earth. Every day, tourism, commerce, and

immigration bring throngs of foreign visitors and returning citizens to our airports, seaports, and land border crossings.

> The political reality is that we don't have the charge to do
> something before it starts, but the longer it unfolds, the
> costlier it gets. Besides, we're still not generating political
> will to end Rwanda – look at the DRC. We do it with ter-
> rorists but not *genocidaires*? Why? National Interest.
>
> Michael Bailey, military advisor to Presidential Special Envoy
> Anthony Lake, 1998-2000

Many of the experts consulted for the W21 Project emphasized
the need to broaden the concept of national interests to include
global security as an integral component of national security. This concept is gaining increasing traction in US and Canadian governmental circles. The Center for American Progress
is a good example of a think tank engaging members of the US
Congress and the public to promote "sustainable security," the
concept that using foreign aid as a strategic tool to strengthen
weak states is a means of protecting the United States from the
national security threats posed by failing or failed states. Within
this broadened framework of what constitutes the national interest, policy makers are encouraged to develop a foreign policy
that affirms the connections between political, economic, social,
health, and environmental issues. It is imperative that the US and
Canadian governments adopt a holistic approach and use all the
instruments of soft and hard power at their disposal to reduce
risks to human security at home and abroad. In order to succeed
in this endeavor, governments must focus on the prevention of
mass atrocities, paying particular attention to high-risk countries
and regions.

While some policy makers understand that the process of
globalization has transformed crises in regions once considered
remote into problems with potentially serious security consequences, surprisingly few political leaders have recommended

making these issues top priorities. Decision makers should consider the prevention of regional destabilization and social upheaval – the long-term consequences of mass atrocities – as vital to the national interest.

In today's globalized world, citizens of the United States and Canada are increasingly organizing themselves to influence policy makers in Washington and Ottawa, a development reflected in the rapid multiplication over the past two decades of NGOs working on human rights and humanitarian relief. The growing strength of NGOs in liberal democracies presents new opportunities to mobilize domestic political will.

We must persuade leaders that a modern definition of the national interest requires a greater emphasis on the prevention of mass atrocities. To this end, a focus on prevention involves an examination of the drivers of deadly violence that create the conditions of instability where mass atrocities are more likely to occur. The combined force of these drivers must be addressed through sustainable preventive measures in order to fulfill the mandate of the first pillar of R2P – the responsibility to prevent.

## DRIVERS OF DEADLY VIOLENCE

The changing global landscape frames W21's argument that the prevention of mass atrocities needs to be deeply integrated into American and Canadian foreign policy. Our intention in the following discussion is to underline the structural changes taking place across the world that will require both countries to become more engaged in humanitarian interventions in the future.

Crimes against humanity and genocidal killings are threats to global security and have remained all-too prevalent since the onset of the twenty-first century. No single factor causes crimes against humanity and genocide; they are propelled by a complex web of factors that act as drivers to produce the most deadly forms of violence against civilians. Within policy circles, there is a growing understanding that mass atrocities result from the convergence of long-term structural factors such as endemic poverty and more proximate causes such as economic crises and opportunistic political demagoguery. The drivers of deadly violence identified here serve to highlight some of the primary destabilizing factors whose combined impact increases the risk of mass atrocities. Although not an exhaustive list, these drivers should be incorporated into any analysis designed to identify high-risk situations.

We have identified poverty and inequality, population growth and the "youth bulge," ethnic nationalism, and climate change as four important drivers of deadly violence. If democratic countries fail to develop and implement a sustainable strategy to prevent mass atrocities, future crises are ever more likely to spiral out of control and destabilize entire countries and regions. Indeed, in an era of unprecedented global interconnectedness political isolationism simply is not a viable policy option. Moreover, if the driving forces of deadly violence are not understood, American and Canadian leaders will continue to simply react to major humanitarian crises without addressing the structural factors that create the breeding ground for mass atrocities.

I think the purpose of Canadian foreign policy should be to save lives, to prevent the loss of life around the world, which means conflict prevention, it means a deep commitment to ending massive poverty among the least well off in the world, and a commitment to fighting climate change, because the climate change crisis is having a direct impact on the human condition. And those three things go together.

Bob Rae, Canadian member of Parliament

### Poverty and inequality

According to the United Nations Development Programme, poor access to basic subsistence necessities such as food, water, and shelter combined with few opportunities for education, employment, and social equality indicate "low human development." Human rights violations, conflict, and mass atrocities are more frequent in countries with the lowest rankings. Without external economic assistance and development support, countries afflicted by poor socio-economic conditions suffer from higher risks of political collapse and rampant violence.

These endemic structural deficiencies not only affect the survival and well-being of civilians but also the durability of state governance. Failed and weak states can arise directly from civil conflict, as in Sudan, or from bad governance, as in Zimbabwe, hindering access to economic opportunities and often resulting in the complete breakdown of the rule of law. In some cases, state failure is a result of unequally apportioning the benefits of globalization, leading to the accumulation of wealth by the few and the deepening of poverty among the many. To lower the likelihood of mass atrocities, it is increasingly important to take a preventive approach and address the structural elements of endemic poverty and inequality through development.

### Population growth and the youth bulge

Another important driver of deadly violence is population growth and the demographic phenomenon referred to as the "youth bulge." Demographers estimate that more than fifty countries will see their populations increase in size by more than thirty per cent within the next two decades. In 2009, the United Nations' Department of Economic and Social Affairs predicted that by 2012 the world's population will exceed seven billion people, and by 2050 it will climb to just over nine billion. This means that within four decades our planet will add the combined equivalent of the current populations of China and India. The Democratic Republic of the Congo, Ethiopia, and Nigeria, in particular, are expected to see significant population growth, in addition to Middle Eastern and Asian countries such as Afghanistan, Pakistan, and Yemen. Rapid population growth will take place mostly in developing countries and will place tremendous pressure on government services, infrastructures, and natural resources. The evidence suggests that in economically weak countries there is a direct relationship between high numbers of youth, political instability, and violence, primarily because these countries are unable to absorb large numbers of young men into the labor force, increasing the potential for social unrest and violence. Many of the "youth bulge" countries are located in sub-Saharan Africa.

## Nationalism

Extreme ethnic nationalism is also a considerable force for genocide and other mass atrocities. History has shown that times of economic difficulty are propitious for the spread of populist rhetoric and, in extreme cases, exclusive nationalism that demonizes outsiders. The most striking example of this phenomenon emerged during the interwar years, from 1919 to 1939, when fascist and Nazi politicians whipped up ethnic nationalism, targeted entrepreneurial minorities, and demonized social groups as scapegoats for economic and societal ills. In the post-Cold War era, the breakup of the former Yugoslavia sparked by ethnic nationalist movements fuelled campaigns of ethnic cleansing in Croatia and Bosnia. In Rwanda, the rise of the Hutu Power movement in the 1990s was partly responsible for radicalizing the population to hate the Tutsi minority and curtailing any viable prospect for peaceful multi-party governance. In the contemporary context, there is reason to fear that the global financial crisis could fuel extreme nationalist movements that might otherwise have remained dormant in countries across the world.

## Climate change

There is a strong consensus among scientists and government officials that climate change is occurring and that this will bring about profound and irreversible changes to the global environment. These projected changes carry broad implications for international security. The earth's tropical and equatorial zones are expected to be hit hardest, with the consequence that poor countries will suffer more than industrialized states located in the temperate zone. For this reason, climate change could ultimately lead to more failed states and an increase in deadly violence.

When you add climate change, the potential for distur-
bances overseas increases substantially. We're dealing
with an equation that has many different variables.

Jim Bishop, vice-president, humanitarian policy and practice,
InterAction

The by-products of climate change include drought, desertification, increasing storm intensity, changing rainfall patterns, and rising sea levels. The likelihood of deadly violence
is more pronounced when societies are faced with resource
scarcity. Increasing desertification and coastal flooding will
force displaced people to migrate in search of agricultural
land and water. Changing rainfall patterns and melting gla-
ciers will result in water scarcity, reducing agricultural production. The world has already experienced the dangerous
consequences of this scenario in Darfur, where conflict began
in 2003 during an ecological crisis. In Darfur, changing rainfall patterns forced people to migrate farther in search of new
grazing land and fights erupted between pastoralists and sed-
entary farmers. Competition for overstretched resources will
no doubt increase, laying the groundwork for new sites of
deadly violence.

### The perfect storm

The combined impact of poverty and inequality, rapid demographic growth, ethnic nationalism, and climate change on international peace and security makes it strategically imperative to
operationalize the principles of *The Responsibility to Protect*
report. These underlying structural factors increase the risks of
mass atrocities perpetrated against civilians and pose a credible
danger to American and Canadian national interests, particularly when weighing the probable high costs of inaction and the
relatively low costs of prevention.

## THE COSTS OF INACTION

The knock-on effects of large-scale mass atrocities in neglected regions of the globe affect security, which includes public health, domestic political legitimacy, and the government balance sheets of Canada and the United States. These costs are incurred when no effective action is undertaken to prevent and respond to mass atrocities. If we want to avoid them, we must grasp the importance in an interdependent world of a preventive and proactive foreign policy.

### Security costs

For national governments, the traditional meaning of security was once reduced to the defense of territorial borders against invasion and attrition. The meaning of "security" has expanded over the course of the last two decades beyond state-centric concerns related to defense. Security challenges now include a wider variety of international and transnational threats affecting states and their citizens.

Inhumanity, when it is systematized as it is in dictatorial and genocidal regimes, is not only an outrage against common human values, but it also carries very real security implications.

Strobe Talbott, president of the Brookings Institution

Failed states inevitably pose a lethal threat to regional stability and international security. As the contemporary history of Somalia and Afghanistan demonstrates, failed states produce serious international security and humanitarian consequences. Instead of working as responsible members of the international community, these states often become safe havens for organized criminal and terrorist gangs, spawning major transnational problems including the disruption of overland trade routes and international shipping lanes.

The emergence of piracy off the coast of East Africa offers a good example of the disruptive effects of failed states. The International Maritime Organization recently reported that global piracy increased by 200 per cent in 2008 compared to the previous year. The US Navy is now patrolling the Somalia coast to safeguard international shipping lanes and Canada deploys naval forces in these same waters as part of NATO's anti-piracy operations. Hijacked cargo ships carrying relief supplies, crude oil, and even Russian T–72 tanks forecast new disasters waiting to unfold.

American and Canadian prosperity depends on the security of the sea lanes, which link ports around the world to those at New York, Los Angeles, Charleston, Long Beach, Norfolk, Houston, Halifax, Montreal, and Vancouver. Seventy per cent of global trade moves through narrow shipping lanes like the Suez Canal and the Gulf of Aden, off the coast of Yemen and Somalia. Accordingly, policy makers are beginning to pay more attention to the nexus between development and security. The efflorescence of piracy is a powerful reminder that the traditional moral imperative to address global poverty through development assistance is vitally connected to the national security interests of the United States and Canada.

The outbreak of infectious disease also poses security risks to populations around the globe. Violent conflict and the breakdown of law and order dramatically increase the potential for the spread of contagious diseases. Mass atrocities generate internal and external displacement raising the overall risk of epidemics.

In situations in which civilians have been driven off their land, agriculture is routinely disrupted, reducing food production and increasing the risk of famine. Famine and food shortages erode resistance to disease, further increasing the risk of epidemics. Infectious diseases spread like wildfire after conflict destroys key public utilities, especially water purification and pumping facilities, while attacks on health care infrastructure further impair the ability to combat disease outbreaks. Displaced civilians often have no choice but to seek protection and shelter in

overcrowded, unsanitary camps. Making matters worse, vaccination programs must often be curtailed or suspended in the
midst of mass atrocities.

Some of the epidemic diseases that have re-emerged in Africa
are threatening to spread worldwide. For instance, epidemic
typhus reappeared in Burundi in 1997 after a twelve-year
absence, as an indirect consequence of the civil war that began
in 1993. In Zimbabwe, failed economic policies and incompe-
tent, politically prejudiced governance directly contributed to
outbreaks of cholera, which killed more than 4,200 people and
infected upwards of 100,000 – making it the deadliest outbreak
of the disease in fifteen years. The cholera epidemic spread from
urban to rural areas within Zimbabwe and threatened to spill
over into neighboring South Africa, Mozambique, Botswana,
and Zambia.

> States that cannot or will not stop internal atrocity crimes
> are the kind of states that cannot or will not stop terror-
> ism, weapons proliferation, drug and people trafficking,
> the spread of health pandemics, and other global risks.
>
> Gareth Evans, co-chair of the International Commission on
> Intervention and State Sovereignty and former foreign minis-
> ter of Australia

The HIV/AIDS epidemic began in Africa and spread quickly
from continent to continent. HIV/AIDS is now the leading killer
in Africa, where more than twenty-three million people are
infected – more than two-thirds of the estimated thirty-five million people infected worldwide. This communicable disease continues to claim new victims, partly due to the use of mass rape
as a weapon of war against innocent civilians. In the Democratic
Republic of the Congo (DRC), organized rape devastates women,
families, and communities, and in Zimbabwe, militias loyal to
President Robert Mugabe routinely use rape to intimidate sup-
porters of the political opposition.

Leaders and policy makers in North America also need to consider the potential health risks that mass atrocities pose to their own populations. While it is understood that civilians who flee violence often fall victim to and spread common communicable diseases, little attention has been paid to the possibility that a neglected humanitarian crisis could evolve into a global pandemic. In the globalized world, connected by intercontinental air travel, commercial shipping, and luxury cruise ships, the costs of not responding to occurrences of mass atrocities in seemingly isolated areas afflicted by the suspension of health care and inoculation programs amidst systematic rape, displacement, and famine may create significant public health threats for residents of the United States and Canada. At the end of the First World War, the 1918–19 influenza pandemic killed between twenty and fifty million people, demonstrating that epidemics erupting in the aftermath of deadly violence can jump far beyond conflict areas. In a very short period of time, such an outbreak can produce multiple waves of epidemics and precipitate global health crises.

THE RIPPLE EFFECTS OF MASS ATROCITIES IN
AMERICAN AND CANADIAN CITIES
Due diligence requires that we do everything possible to prevent mass atrocities in Africa and other parts of the world to maintain our own public health security. Canada and the United States simply cannot afford to stand by and permit vast parts of the world to fall off the public health radar screen. Our consistent failure to reach the UN goal of allocating 0.7 percent of GDP to foreign aid is shameful. Canada's limited funding of international health initiatives that are necessary to control epidemic infectious diseases and to assist in maintaining vaccination programs could come home to haunt us: drug resistant tuberculosis, avian influenza, HIV/AIDS, yellow fever, West Nile virus, malaria … the list of lethal and serious chronic diseases in many parts of the developing world is endless. Genocide and crimes against humanity destroy health infrastructures,

lower the disease resistance of large populations, and displace millions to unsanitary refugee camps. Preventing genocide and crimes against humanity are front-line tasks in our fight to maintain public health security right here in North America. Our politicians and public health officials need to lead in this area.

Jay S. Keystone MD MSC (CTM) FRCPC, Tropical Disease Unit, Toronto General Hospital, professor of medicine, University of Toronto

## *Political costs*

The United States and Canada are mature democracies that guarantee the political and civil rights of their citizens. With the continued rise of education and global travel, the American and Canadian publics have increasingly expressed their commitment to human rights at home and abroad.

The United States and Canada are also diverse and open societies, which accept a large number of immigrants from around the world. Diaspora communities in North America often assert their cultural, ethnic, religious, and national identities within their adopted countries and have become increasingly active lobbyists for domestic and foreign policy priorities. New communications technologies allow immigrants to retain ties to their homeland through foreign language Internet news and television programming. Moreover, diaspora communities can be mobilized into influential political forces. In March 2009, more than 120,000 members of the Sri Lankan Tamil diaspora in Toronto protested against the policies of the Sri Lankan state towards Tamil civilians. Their protest demonstration paralyzed downtown Toronto – the financial hub of Canada – and they demanded that the Canadian government pressure the Sri Lankan government to halt its military operations. In May 2009, this group sustained protests on Parliament Hill for weeks and shut down a major highway in downtown Toronto.

Although the degree of political influence and organization within different immigrant communities varies, many have emerged as political forces capable of influencing foreign policy through demonstrations, lobbying, campaign donations, and voting in elections. As Canadian and American cities become more cosmopolitan, politicians are increasingly reaching out to communities with strong cultural, ethnic, and religious identities for electoral and campaign support. Political leaders who pay attention to the concerns of the diaspora communities will reap rewards; politicians who do not will pay a price at election time. In the years ahead, diaspora groups will play an increasing role in advocacy campaigns designed to mobilize the will to intervene. If governments do not strengthen their genocide prevention policies, advocates will make the political consequences clear. Public office holders who dismiss mass atrocities because they do not fit easily into the traditional national interest "checklist" will be compelled to consider the devastating consequences of inaction, not only for the victims of mass atrocities but also to maintain electoral support.

### Financial costs

A belated, reactive approach to mass atrocities costs American and Canadian taxpayers much more than anticipatory preventive action would. The Carnegie Commission on Preventing Deadly Conflict estimates that the international community spent more than US$130 billion during the 1990s to respond to crises in a reactive manner. The commission concluded that costly interventions involving the use of military force, such as in Bosnia and Haiti, could have been averted by preventive action.

Following the end of the Rwandan Genocide in 1994, the US Government mounted a large humanitarian assistance program, which, between 1994 and 1996, cost US taxpayers more than US$750 million. David Hamburg has pointed out that this figure was almost equal to the US Agency for International Development's (USAID) annual budget for the entire African continent. The fact that the funds were taken from USAID's existing budget suggests that other US development activities had to be downsized, postponed, or abandoned as a result. Washington's delayed reaction to the Rwandan Genocide ultimately undermined US development strategies and cost taxpayers more money in the long term than would have been the case had the United States acted earlier to prevent this tragedy.

The economic costs of intervention are always higher once mass atrocities are underway. More than fifteen years after the Rwandan Genocide ended, the spillover of mass atrocities into the DRC continues to set back the progress of peace and security in the Great Lakes region of Africa. The Mission of the United Nations Organization in the Democratic Republic of the Congo (MONUC) has the largest annual peacekeeping budget in the world, exceeding US$1.4 billion in 2009. The United States' share of the MONUC budget was estimated at approximately US$300 million in 2008. Relief costs are also mounting in Sudan. Between 2004 and 2009, the United States allocated US$4.6 billion for emergency assistance to victims of the crisis in Darfur. While displaced civilians have benefited from this assistance, the root causes of the conflict in Darfur remain unaddressed through the delivery of humanitarian assistance alone. Consequently, carnage and suffering continues and the violence has spilled over into Chad and the Central African Republic.

Recognizing the financial benefits of prevention and early action will not transform policy making overnight within the foreign policy apparatuses of the United States and Canada, nor will all government officials be swayed by the financial argument in isolation. The real problem is that the US and Canadian government systems have not been designed to make prevention a fundamental component of foreign policy. Leadership within government and pressure from outside the public sector by citizens and NGOs must converge if we are to effect serious changes, such as creating a genocide prevention center at the heart of government.

### The end of inaction

By continuing to drag our feet when prevention is required, we risk watching more crises turn into catastrophes. The twenty-first century challenge of protecting innocent civilians from mass atrocities and the consequences of those atrocities requires a determined decision by senior government leaders in the United States and Canada. Leaders must revise outdated policies, develop new approaches, and increase national capacities to intervene effectively and constructively. We ignore these key lessons at our peril.

The case for the prevention of genocide and crimes against humanity once rested largely on moral imperatives and upholding international treaties and conventions. Despite the UN Convention for the Prevention and Punishment of the Crime of Genocide, and the Geneva Convention and its additional protocols, these arguments have not carried sufficient weight to overwhelm the cold statecraft calculations that have traditionally informed the national interest. In today's unstable and interdependent global environment, the historic national interest approach to foreign policy is no longer effective. The costs of not acting demand serious reflection by the president of the United States and the prime minister of Canada. If the United States and Canada continue to do too little in the face of looming genocides, they will confront more than just their moral failure to save lives; inevitably, they will face long-term security, political, and financial burdens.

US and Canadian leaders now have an opportunity to bring genocide prevention into the public policy lexicon. The work ahead may be daunting, but this book offers leaders a focused set of strategic preventive measures and designated new government offices to address these challenges and provide solutions. And if extra prodding proves necessary, W21 outlines the ways we can pressure US and Canadian decision makers to take the lead early in the crucial sphere of preventing mass atrocities.

Table # 1
No political party in Washington or Ottawa has a monopoly on indifference to
mass atrocities

| Crime | Period | US Leader in Elected Office | Canadian Leader in Elected Office |
|---|---|---|---|
| Armenian Genocide | 1915–18 | Democratic President Woodrow Wilson | Conservative Prime Minister Robert Borden |
| Holocaust | 1938–45 | Democratic President Franklin D. Roosevelt | Liberal Prime Minister William Lyon Mackenzie King |
| Cambodian Genocide | 1975–79 | Republican President Gerald Ford Democratic President James Carter | Liberal Prime Minister Pierre Elliott Trudeau |
| Rwandan Genocide | 1994 | Democratic President William Clinton | Liberal Prime Minister Jean Chrétien |
| Srebrenica Genocide | 1995 | Democratic President William Clinton | Liberal Prime Minister Jean Chrétien |
| Darfur Mass Atrocities | 2003–present | Republican President George W. Bush Democratic President Barack Obama | Liberal Prime Minister Paul Martin Conservative Prime Minister Stephen Harper |

# PART TWO

# Case Studies of the Rwandan Genocide and the Kosovo Crisis

It's one of the two or three things I regret most about my presidency. By the time we thought of doing something about it, it was over... I don't think we could have saved 800,000 lives [in Rwanda ... but] I think I might have saved 250,000 to 400,000. And that's something I have to live with for the rest of my life.

Bill Clinton, former US president, speaking on 29 May 2009 in Toronto, Canada, as cited in Brown, "A Presidential Showdown."

The case studies that follow analyze how US and Canadian deci-sion makers responded to the 1994 Rwandan Genocide and the 1999 Kosovo crisis. W21 studied policy-making processes in Washington and Ottawa to locate political pressure points and discover what NGOs, the media, and civil servants must do to generate political will when humanitarian interventions are essential. The lessons learned from our case studies on these defining crises of the 1990s inform the policy recommendations presented in Part Three.

W21's historical analyses are drawn largely from interviews conducted with American and Canadian politicians, senior gov-ernment officials, NGO representatives, journalists, and academ-ics with direct decision-making experience or expert knowledge on the crises in Rwanda and Kosovo. We interviewed more than eighty people, some for the first time on record, leading us to a nuanced understanding of the American and Canadian responses. To our great regret, a small number of very senior American and Canadian politicians, political aides, and government officials deeply involved in these crises declined our repeated interview requests. While our case studies contribute to a better understanding of what went on behind the scenes in Washington and Ottawa, some important questions remain unanswered, especially concerning the Rwandan Genocide.

## UNITED STATES' DECISION MAKING

### The Rwandan Genocide

Beginning shortly after the First World War, Belgian colonial rule in Rwanda hardened ethnic and socio-economic divisions between the Hutu, Tutsi, and Twa peoples by promoting Tutsi political hegemony. This policy of official ethnic differentiation began with the introduction of identity cards in 1931.[1] In the late 1950s, the exigencies of decolonization and looming elections led Belgian rulers to integrate the Hutu majority into the political power structure – a decision that led to the Hutu Revolution in 1959.

Ethnic tensions between and within the now independent states of Rwanda and Burundi sharply increased. Violence targeting ethnic Tutsis in Rwanda forced 10,000 to flee to neighbouring countries.[2] From 1961 to 1967, numerous rebel groups comprised of ethnic Tutsi refugees attempted ten incursions into Rwanda, all of which failed, resulting in further government retaliation against ethnic Tutsis in the country.[3] These attacks resulted in the deaths of over 20,000 Tutsis and the displacement of 300,000 others who fled Rwanda and sought refuge in bordering countries. In Burundi, the Tutsi-dominated military regime increasingly targeted the country's educated Hutu minority and perpetrated the 1972 massacre of approximately 200,000 Hutus, an action that resulted in an influx of Hutu refugees to Rwanda.[4] In 1973, Juvénal Habyarimana, a Hutu, led a coup and assumed the presidency of Rwanda on a platform of national unity, creating a single-party state dominated by Hutus in 1975.

In 1987 the Rwanda Alliance for National Union, which had been formed in 1979 as a political organization for Tutsi refugees and to advocate for their right to return to Rwanda, was transformed and renamed the Rwanda Patriotic Front (RPF).[5] In 1990, the RPF under the leadership of Paul Kagame invaded Rwanda from Uganda, which intensified both official and popular anti-Tutsi sentiment.[6] This development partly informed Habyarimana's decision in 1992 to incorporate the extremist Hutu political organization, the Coalition for the Defense of the Republic, into Rwanda's multi-party coalition government. In July 1992, the Rwandan government and the RPF signed a ceasefire agreement in Arusha, Tanzania, calling for the creation of a broad-based transitional government.[7] Following a breakdown in the talks and a brief RPF offensive, negotiations were renewed in April 1993, and the Rwandan Government and the RPF asked the United Nations to create a neutral international force to monitor the Arusha Accords, which were signed on 4 August 1993. The UN Security Council subsequently established the United Nations Assistance Mission for Rwanda (UNAMIR) as a Chapter VI peacekeeping operation in October 1993.[8] Led by Canadian Brig.-Gen. Roméo Dallaire, UNAMIR's mandate limited its soldiers to monitoring the peace accords and restricted their use of force to cases of self-defence.[9]

*The Arusha Peace Process*

Throughout the thirteen-month Arusha peace process that began in June 1992, the United States contributed crucial "technical understanding" and dispute negotiation skills, which it had applied to conflicts in Mozambique, Ethiopia-Eritrea, Namibia, and Angola.[10] In addition, the United States provided strategic guidance on the creation of a coalition government with power-sharing arrangements and amalgamated militaries, working to reduce the possibility of renewed civil war. One senior US Government source comments: "We did not have massive strategic interests there. We had to be very deferential towards those who had a much larger interest, including the French, and we maintained that position in Arusha. We did not intend to assert ourselves as leading the process."[11] Rwanda was perceived as lacking exploitable resources and as being peripheral to the geostrategic interests of the United States. Consequently, the diplomatic interactions between the two countries were cordial and characterized chiefly by a donor-recipient foreign aid relationship.[12] According to Herman J. "Hank" Cohen, assistant secretary of state for Africa from 1989 to 1993, Angola and Ethiopia were higher priorities for the United States than Rwanda and the Arusha peace process.[13]

UNAMIR was deployed in October 1993 to monitor the implementation of the Arusha Accords.[14] US support of the mission was largely contingent upon the mission's limited Chapter VI mandate. The decision to support UNAMIR was also influenced by pressure from Rwandan Tutsis and Hutus, who traveled to major US cities to lobby for the UN operation.[15] Many American officials viewed the initial peacekeeping mission in Rwanda as an "easy win" that would quell the voices calling for reduced US involvement in UN peacekeeping operations.[16] Although violence continued in Rwanda, provoked particularly over the composition of the transitional government, the US Government continued to assert the sustainability of the Arusha Accords. When Hank Cohen left his position in the State Department in April 1993, a few months before the signing of the Arusha Accords, he recalls that he "did not consider a non-implementation scenario."[17] As the new assistant secretary of state for Africa, George Moose recalls, the State Department focused on the negotiations.[18] Prudence Bushnell, former deputy assistant secretary for Africa, confirms the US emphasis on the political peace process.[19] "The United States put a huge policy emphasis on the Arusha Accords," explains Bushnell.[20] "There is a profound lesson for me as a policy maker, in that you can be so focused on your policy that you have blinders on."[21]

In its blind commitment to the peace process, the State Department overstated the capacity of the Arusha peace process to stop the violence. "We saw the peace accords ... as the ultimate solution to ongoing tensions and to assassinations, to killings that we knew were ongoing," Bushnell reflects.[22] In Washington and Kigali, US officials did not consider genocide as a possibility. David Rawson, US ambassador to Rwanda, explains: "I felt that, if we went back into open conflict, it would be a very brutal and bloody kind of thing. I didn't think necessarily there would be genocide."[23]

### Somalia and PDD–25

In 1992, the US-led, UN-sanctioned mission in Somalia, the United Task Force, succeeded in providing humanitarian aid to hundreds of thousands of Somali civilians and broke the back of the famine. However, the more ambitious, second phase UN-led operation, UNOSOM II, which included the goal of "nation-building," isolated key clan leaders and led to the killing of twenty-four Pakistani peacekeepers. In retaliation, the United States attempted to apprehend warlord Mohammed Farrah Aideed, which ended with the tragic deaths of eighteen American Rangers in Mogadishu in October 1993.[24] The American public's reaction to the killings, combined with congressional outrage, convinced the Clinton administration to order the withdrawal of US military personnel within six months. Sarah Sewall, deputy assistant secretary for peacekeeping and humanitarian assistance at the Department of Defense, recalls that in the early days of the Clinton administration, the White House was committed to working with the United Nations to support multilateral interventions.[25] To this end, Sewall and several members of the National Security Council (NSC) were tasked with creating a coherent peacekeeping policy. This culminated in a draft presidential review decision, PRD–13, allowing greater US troop involvement under UN command.[26] However, Sewall asserts that the Pentagon had little interest in peacekeeping operations and provided little support for PRD–13.[27]

Following the killing of the US Rangers in Somalia and congressional objections to PRD–13, the Clinton administration reversed its policy from assertive multilateralism to selective engagement.[28] This policy shift was outlined in a presidential decision directive, PDD–25, setting restrictive criteria for US involvement in multilateral peacekeeping operations. The restrictions included limiting US military participation to Chapter VI peacekeeping missions essential to advancing vital US interests. James Woods, former deputy assistant secretary for African affairs at the Department of Defense, argues that the Somalia debacle deeply influenced the wording of PDD–25, which was designed to "narrow the possibility that we [the US] would get engaged [and] ... crystallized a growing body of resistance to these types of potentially dangerous humanitarian interventions."[29] In contrast, high-level NSC officials, such as former national security advisor Anthony Lake, assert the restrictions in PDD–25 were adopted as a means of "protecting" traditional peacekeeping against attack.[30] As Lake states, "we had to be able to demonstrate that we were doing it [peacekeeping] in a careful, effective, practical way. That's what PDD–25 was about."[31]

In reality, PDD–25 blocked efforts to expand peacekeeping to include the protection of civilians and directly limited the US response to the Rwandan Genocide. As Prudence Bushnell reflects: "I mean, the criterion was, 'Don't engage in peacekeeping unless there's peace.' Essentially, it [PDD–25] was just such strict criteria and you have to have an exit strategy. Hah! Would those criteria still be our policy today? It was clear that the interagency did not want us to engage in a peacekeeping operation in Rwanda."[32]

### Warnings of genocide

Prior to the eruption of genocide in April 1994, the United States received a significant volume of intelligence warning of plans for large-scale massacres. In particular, the American embassy in Kigali informed Washington of hate speech broadcasts on Radio Milles Collines, arms trafficking, and the training of youth extremists.[33] On 11 January 1994, UNAMIR Force Commander Brigadier General Roméo Dallaire cabled information to the UN Department of Peacekeeping Operations about an "extermination" plot to kill Tutsis and shared this information with the diplomatic corps in Kigali. David Rawson recalled a briefing at a foreign embassy in Kigali in which Dallaire informed the Americans of "a collection of arms, stocking of arms, and the distribution of arms to civilian elements."[34]

Following a request from Dallaire, Rawson forwarded the intelligence to the State Department in Washington.[35] It is

unclear how widely the intelligence was distributed but it was
brought to the attention of Political Military Advisor Tony Marley. However, Marley says he perceived Dallaire as a "neophyte"
and "questioned whether he knew what he was talking about."[36]
    Marley contends that since 1992 he had heard predictions
of looming mass killings in Rwanda, but they had never taken
place "on a scale larger than several hundreds of people."[37] Dallaire's warning was not forwarded to key people in the State
Department's Africa Bureau, including George Moose, the
assistant secretary of state for Africa, or Bushnell, the deputy
assistant secretary of state for Africa. Bushnell maintains that,
"when General Dallaire talks about the memos he sent to the
UN, about arms, and the informant, I got no wind of that from
any of my diplomatic colleagues."[38] Given the constant interaction among the diplomatic corps, Bushnell cannot explain
why the information was not communicated to her: "I never
have figured out why it was that this was not the talk of the diplomatic community."[39] Similarly, John Shattuck, former assistant secretary of state for democracy, human rights and labor,
states that although he received daily intelligence briefings and
was in frequent contact with Bushnell, Moose, and NSC officials
Eric Schwartz and Don Steinberg, he did not see the Dallaire
cable. "I had never seen the Dallaire cable," he asserts.[40] "I
didn't know anything about that."[41]

*Government awareness of genocide*

On 6 April 1994, following the death of Rwandan President
Juvénal Habyarimana and the outbreak of violence in Rwanda,
Washington began to plan for the evacuation of its nationals.
Bushnell informed Secretary of State Warren Christopher of the
likelihood of "widespread violence" and of the likely necessity of
evacuating American nationals.[42] Bushnell explains that Washington saw "utter anarchy" in Rwanda and that "nobody really
knew who was in charge or what was happening."[43]
    The government immediately assembled a task force of offi-
cials from the Pentagon and the State Department to coordinate
the evacuation of Americans.[44] According to Bushnell, the evacuation of US nationals was the State Department's top priority.

"I was focused 100 per cent on getting Americans out."[45] On 10 April, 258 Americans were evacuated by land.[46] Joyce Leader, second in command at the US Embassy, was among the last American officials to leave Kigali. Leader had tried unsuccessfully to hide Rwanda's prime minister, Agathe Uwilingiyimana, in her house before the presidential guard killed the prime minister and the ten Belgian peacekeepers guarding her.

On 8 April 1994, the Operations Center of the Executive Secretariat of the State Department distributed a confidential situation report to the CIA, the joint chiefs of staff, the national security advisor, the secretary of defense, and the State Department. The report described the violence in Kigali as "fighting between the RPF and Rwandan military" and mapped out a plan for the evacuation of Americans but failed to mention the systematic killing of Rwanda's ethnic Tutsis.[47] On the same day, the CIA's National Intelligence Daily report stated that, "Hutu security elements from the Presidential Guard, the gendarmerie, and the military killed several government officials – including the Prime Minister – took at least two hostages and killed numerous Tutsi civilians in Kigali."[48] Fighting had broken out between the RPF and the Rwandan Army in northern Rwanda and around Kigali due to the targeted killing of Tutsi civilians and political moderates. However, during the first few days of the genocide it was not clear to policy makers in Washington that the Rwandan military and the Interahamwe – the extremist Hutu youth militia – were slaughtering ethnic Tutsis and Hutu political moderates in a politically motivated plot orchestrated by Hutu extremists within the Rwandan government.[49]

Following the evacuation of American nationals from Rwanda to Bujumbura, Burundi, US Ambassador Rawson telephoned the Rwanda interagency task force in Washington DC, as protocol required. When Rawson phoned, President Bill Clinton was unexpectedly visiting the task force's operations room at the State Department. The president spoke to Rawson, congratulating him on the successful evacuation, and asked Rawson to brief him upon his return to the United States.[50] Upon Rawson's return to Washington later in April, he attempted to meet with President Clinton but to no avail. "The president invited me to

come to the White House, and then once I got back, the people
who were in communication with the White House tried to make
that happen, and it didn't happen."[51] Rawson asserts that had
he met with Clinton, he would have advised him to support the
UNAMIR operation and the requests put forward by the Force
Commander, Brigadier-General Dallaire.[52] Instead, the United
States relinquished its support for UNAMIR, indirectly encouraging international withdrawal from Rwanda.

For the American and Belgian governments, the brutal murder
of UNAMIR peacekeepers brought back memories of the eighteen Rangers killed in Somalia. The false parallels made between
these two UN operations ultimately informed the Belgian and
American decisions to push for the total withdrawal of UNAMIR:
Washington and Brussels believed that there was no longer a
peace to keep. However, the killing of the ten Belgian peacekeepers in Rwanda did not immediately trigger a withdrawal. On 8
April 1994, one day after the murder of the Belgian peacekeepers,
a State Department situation report stated that "the Belgian PM
asked Boutros-Ghali to strengthen the UN contingent. The Belgian government wants enhanced equipment and/or firepower ...
The Belgians are willing to keep their UNAMIR troops in Rwanda
after the planned evacuation, but cannot provide more troops."[53]

At a Peacekeeping Core Group meeting on 13 April 1994,
headed by Richard Clarke, special assistant to the president in
the NSC, and attended by officials from the State Department,
the Pentagon, and US intelligence agencies, the US Government decided to pursue a full UNAMIR withdrawal. Douglas
Bennet, assistant secretary for international organizations,
urged Secretary of State Warren Christopher to communicate
the US position for the withdrawal of UNAMIR in an upcoming telephone conversation with UN Secretary-General Boutros
Boutros-Ghali.[54] Following the Peacekeeping Core Group meeting, Bennet advised in a memo that "the chaotic conditions in
Rwanda" made it "impossible for UNAMIR to fulfill its mandate."[55] Bennet wrote: "The onus for withdrawal should not be
placed on the Belgians" and "It is our view, therefore, that the
force should withdraw from the country now."[56] Christopher
subsequently supported the Peacekeeping Core Group decision

without consulting further with the State Department, the secretary of defense, the national security advisor, or the president. Christopher sent a memo to Madeleine Albright, the US ambassador to the United Nations, on 15 April, which stated that, "the United States believes that the first priority of the Security Council is to instruct the Secretary General to implement an orderly withdrawal of all/all UNAMIR forces from Rwanda ... and that we will oppose any effort at this time to preserve a UNAMIR presence in Rwanda."[57]

On 21 April, before Albright headed to the Security Council meeting to vote for a complete withdrawal, she met with Alison Des Forges, a Rwanda expert with Human Rights Watch, and her colleague, Monique Mujawamariya, a Rwandan human rights activist who had just escaped the genocide. Des Forges recalls pleading with Albright: "We said very, very, very explicitly, there are at least 20,000 people in the Amahoro stadium. If you withdraw all of the troops, all of those people will be killed and that will be on your head."[58] According to Des Forges, Albright responded: "You have a very powerful message. But you are delivering it to the wrong person."[59] Albright advised Des Forges to meet with National Security Advisor Anthony Lake. "If they refuse you," Albright said, "tell them to call me."[60]

At their meeting with Lake, Des Forges and Mujawamariya argued fervently for retaining UNAMIR, but were told that they did not represent a sufficiently important political constituency to force the government to change its position.[61] "He just said, 'Make more noise. We listen to noise,'" Des Forges recalls.[62] Kenneth Roth, director of Human Rights Watch, dismissed this justification: "It's a cheap excuse. It's basically saying force us to do it because we're not going to take the political risks involved to do the right thing on our own."[63]

Madeleine Albright called the National Security Council in Washington and argued with Richard Clarke over the withdrawal order.[64] Albright says she felt she would "get a better hearing" through the National Security Council, but Clarke told her to follow her instructions.[65] "I screamed into the phone. I said, 'They're unacceptable. I want them changed,'" Albright recalls.[66] After the NSC told her to "chill out and calm down," they sent her new instructions and allowed her to support the decision to maintain 270 UNAMIR troops, a symbolic UN force that remained in Kigali throughout the genocide.[67]

Roger Winter, head of the US Committee for Refugees, an NGO, had just left Rwanda for south Sudan when Habyarimana's plane was shot down. "I went and began to spend much of May and June [1994] travelling with the Rwandan Patriotic Front as they rolled into the country. I would generally be there for about ten days, go back to Washington and there would be meetings set up for me to brief the intelligence wings of the Defense Department and the State Department and, of course, the CIA. Sometimes the meetings would be held in either one of those buildings. They were organized by the Defense Intelligence Agency folks. I'm not sure how many back and forth trips there were before the hostilities actually ended, but I felt very clearly that I knew what the system knew ... It was for that reason, in particular, that we were so incensed by the lack of action on the part of the administration."[68] Winter provided the officials with "on-the-ground findings" and photographic evidence of the atrocities.[69] "People in the system knew exceedingly clearly what was happening."[70]

By early May 1994, congressional advocates also added to the pressure bearing down on the White House. On 4 May, the chairman of the Congressional Black Caucus, Kweisi Mfume, and Congressman Donald Payne sent a letter to President Clinton informing him of the Congressional Black Caucus's concern over Rwanda and the need for the White House to pay more attention to the atrocities occurring there.[71] A response had still not been received on 16 June, when the caucus sent a second letter, criticizing the Clinton administration's slow action on Rwanda.[72] The Congressional Black Caucus remained critical of US policy toward Rwanda. It boycotted the White House Conference on Africa in June and on 1 July requested a meeting with President Clinton.[73] On 26 July President Clinton finally met with Donald Payne just before the congressman's trip to Rwanda with Secretary of Defense William Perry to oversee the US provision of humanitarian relief. However, Payne's meeting with Clinton took place well after the genocide had ended.[74]

Senator Paul Simon, chairman of the Senate Foreign Relations subcommittee on Africa, phoned Dallaire in Kigali on 13 May to gain insight from the field, while Senator Jim Jeffords called for US military intervention to stop the massacres.[75] The two senators delivered a letter to the White House on 13 May calling for action but the president did not respond until 9 June.[76] In his response, Clinton reiterated his position that the government must strive to secure a ceasefire in order to halt the killings but stopped short of proposing any action to protect civilians or halt the genocide.[77]

The issue of jamming hate radio station RTLM also elicited congressional pressure. On 5 May, Undersecretary of Defense Frank Wisner had reported to Sandy Berger that jamming the RTLM hate radio would be ineffective and too expensive.[78] Wisner wrote that the Commando Solo C–130 aircraft, the Department of Defense jamming platform, "costs approximately US$8,500 per flight hour and requires a semi-secure flight area of operations due to its vulnerability and limited self-protection."[79] The United States also maintained that jamming radios could affect its diplomatic relations with Rwanda.[80] Yet in 1991, the US operation in Haiti included jamming hate radio and no one raised such objections.[81] On 1 June 1994, Senator Ted Kennedy wrote a letter requesting that Secretary of State Christopher pursue the jamming of hate radio broadcasts in Rwanda to stop the incitement of violence. The State Department replied that it would not pursue the option because it presented legal problems and would incur a high financial cost.[82] A year after the genocide ended, Tony Marley suggested that the United States could have blown up the RTLM radio transmitter or its antenna with a few pounds of plastic explosives – a relatively inexpensive and feasible operation that could have interrupted the communications of the *genocidaires*.[83] Marley regretted that there was no will to act covertly.[84] No "soft options," which might have mitigated the genocide, were given serious consideration by the US Government.

## Media failure

With few exceptions, the national media failed to report accurately on the carnage unfolding in Rwanda in April 1994. The

lack of media attention reduced pressure on the US Government
to propose robust action at the critical 21 April Security Council meeting, where it voted to withdraw the bulk of UNAMIR's
troops. American television news paid only "modest" attention
to the story during the most deadly initial three months of the
genocide.[85] *The Washington Post* and *The New York Times* both
featured front-page stories on Rwanda on 9 and 10 April that
described the death of President Habyarimana and the occur-
rence of political "executions."[86]

*Time* and *Newsweek* first mentioned Rwanda on 18 April
1994, but the story did not make the cover of *Time* until 16 May
and, like most media reports, it misrepresented the massacres as
instances of "tribal" conflict.[87] The description of the violence
as a component of an ongoing civil war or ancient tribal conflict sublimated the extraordinary horror of the mass murder of
civilians. Alan J. Kuperman notes that although the situation in
Rwanda was "legitimately confusing" in April, the media failed
to fulfill its role as a "surrogate early-warning system."[88] Consequently, the American public remained ill-informed about the
genocide and the diplomatic and military options available to
halt it.

American news coverage increased in May, thanks to the presence of many American television crews in South Africa where
they were covering the national elections. As a clearer picture
emerged about the genocide, television crews were reassigned to
Rwanda. "As investigators try to make sense of the killing," ABC
correspondent Ron Allen reported on 7 May, "there is more evidence Rwanda's massacres may be a premeditated political act,
not a spontaneous eruption of ethnic hatred."[89] Roméo Dallaire
notes that this increase in media coverage during the first half of
May influenced members of the UN Security Council to approve
a mandate for UNAMIR II on 17 May.[90] "I think it was wear and
tear by media, the continuing of the genocide, and the realization
that this goddamn thing wasn't ending."[91]

The news media's pressure for action arrived too late, however, and even then few accounts emphasized the genocide. The
media only covered the tragedy in Rwanda in earnest when the
story of the refugee crisis emerged in May 1994 and US television

correspondents reported the spread of disease and the rate of death in the refugee camps.[92] In *The Path of a Genocide*, contributors Steven Livingston and Todd Eachus conclude that the media's emphasis on the humanitarian crisis enabled the Clinton administration to distance itself from the genocide and policy options for intervention.[93] "If there was a 'CNN effect,' it came in response to this second story," Livingston and Eachus write.[94] "The [Clinton] administration was quite ready to employ Pentagon resources in a 'feeding and watering' operation, as it was commonly referred to at the Pentagon. What it was not willing to do, and would not allow television pictures to force it to do, was to stop the slaughter early on."[95]

### The 'g-word' debate

In April and May of 1994, a debate ensued in Washington concerning the legal ramifications of describing the killings in Rwanda as "genocide." Some feared that use of the term would necessitate intervention under the Genocide Convention, despite the fact that, as of mid-April, many in government understood that the massacres fit the legal definition. Former Defense Intelligence Agency analyst Rick Orth recalls that daily interagency meetings attended by senior National Security Council officials included intelligence updates on Rwanda; and on at least one occasion, a member of the Pentagon's Directorate for Intelligence personally delivered information about the genocide to the White House.[96]

John Shattuck made a fact-finding trip to Rwanda at the end of April with the help of Peter Tarnoff, undersecretary of state for political affairs. After observing the genocide first hand and returning to Washington on 9 May, he pushed others in government to describe the massacres as genocide.[97] Despite Shattuck's efforts, the State Department only went so far as to describe the killings as "acts of genocide" – a decision illustrating how verbal nuance was used to curtail action.[98] This strategy was outlined explicitly in a 1 May discussion paper from the office of the secretary of defense, which warned, "Be Careful. Legal at State was worried about this yesterday – Genocide finding could commit the USG to actually 'do something.'"[99]

The Defense Intelligence Agency produced an intelligence instruction cable on 9 May, outlining parallel, separate violence in both the Rwandan civil war and the genocide. "It appears that, in addition to the random massacres of Tutsis by Hutu militias and individuals, there is an organized, parallel effort of genocide being implemented by the army to destroy the leadership of the Tutsi community. The original intent was to kill only the political elite supporting reconciliation; however, the government lost control of the militias, and the massacre spread like wildfire. It continues to rage out of control."[100]

Although the cable acknowledged genocide, it mistakenly explained that the Hutu political elite intended "politicide," or the destruction of the Tutsi political elite. In reality, Hutu political extremists in the government of Rwanda orchestrated the genocide.[101] Rick Orth acknowledges that he was aware that the intelligence report in early May did not accurately describe the killings taking place in Rwanda.[102] Orth submitted his comments on the outgoing instruction cable to indicate that genocide was occurring in Rwanda, but the Defense Intelligence Agency's Mideast Africa Section and the J5 Strategic Plans and Policy division of the joint chiefs of staff responded that the comments arrived thirty minutes too late to be incorporated into the official cable.[103] US officials feared that using the term "genocide" would encourage "mission creep," and pull the United States into the conflict in Rwanda. In a 20 May memo to Secretary Christopher, State Department officials acknowledged the existence of genocide but urged the use of the phrase "acts of genocide" to insulate the United States from legal obligations under the Genocide Convention.[104] The memo stated: "A USG statement that acts of genocide have occurred would not have any particular legal consequences" and "Although lacking in legal consequences, a clear statement that the USG believes that acts of genocide have occurred could increase pressure for USG activism in response to the crisis in Rwanda."[105] In an effort to frame US policy as legitimate, the State Department advised the government to "seize the opportunity to ... use the genocide label to condemn events in Rwanda." Otherwise, "our credibility will be undermined with human rights groups and the general public, who may question how much evidence we can legitimately require before coming to a policy conclusion."[106]

On 21 May, Secretary of State Christopher authorized State Department officials to use the word "genocide" at the UN Human Rights Commission.[107] The authorization did not extend to other forums or public statements. According to instructions from Christopher three days later, State Department officials were authorized to support a resolution at the commission indicating that "genocide" or "acts of genocide" were occurring in Rwanda, but they were not authorized to characterize independent incidents in the country as genocide.[108] After sustained questions from journalists about the number of "acts of genocide" it takes to constitute "genocide," Christopher succumbed to media pressure in June 1994, when he told reporters: "If there is any particular magic in calling it genocide, I have no hesitancy in saying that."[109]

Jared Cohen, author of a scholarly study on US policy towards the Rwandan Genocide, asserts that the debate over the term "genocide," which overshadows humanitarian crises, is "completely meaningless and constitutes a misreading of the Genocide Convention."[110] Cohen explains: "It's ironic that a convention that was designed to have diction used to encourage states to intervene actually became the most valuable tool for nations to justify not intervening."[111]

### United States takes late action

After the controversial deployment of French troops for Opération Turquoise on 23 June 1994, the Clinton administration began to take action. Operation Provide Comfort signaled a dramatic – though fatally belated – shift in the American response to Rwanda. The United States had stalled the expansion of UNAMIR at the Security Council, instead proposing a humanitarian operation along Rwanda's borders to provide "safe havens" for refugees.[112] A "two-stage solution" was proposed whereby armored personnel carriers and more than 800 Ghanaian peacekeepers would be deployed, with further peacekeepers arriving following a ceasefire.[113] The RPF opposed the intervention and threatened to use force against new UN peacekeepers, and by mid-July the

RPF had defeated the remnants of the Rwandan military and declared a unilateral ceasefire.[114]

Media coverage of the refugee crisis rose in July and generated an outpouring of international aid. The genocide had ended and camps were set up on the border of eastern Zaire. Clinton pledged 4,000 American troops to aid in the humanitarian relief effort and urged Congress to authorize US$170 million for emergency relief, a figure that almost doubled in the next few months.[115] In the course of this operation, American troops were deployed to Entebbe in Uganda to provide logistical support and Goma in Zaire to work on halting the spread of cholera. A few hundred American troops were deployed to Kigali in Rwanda but they remained stationed at Kigali airport.[116] Clinton proved less averse to sending American troops to Rwanda to assist in the provision of post-genocide humanitarian aid than to providing security to civilians threatened with mass murder.

The US failure to thwart mass atrocities in Rwanda in 1994 differs greatly from US action in Kosovo in 1998–99. In the former case, Washington blocked American involvement in peacekeeping by avoiding diplomatic options and refusing to describe the crisis in Rwanda as "genocide." In the latter case, the United States' experience with Milosevic's brutal record in the Balkans, and its perceived national interest in securing Europe, solidified its continued and incremental action to halt ethnic cleansing. Although NATO's military intervention remains highly controversial, Kosovo stands as a decisive case showcasing the multiple types of "soft" and "hard" interventions that can be undertaken by the US Government to thwart mass atrocities.

### The Kosovo Crisis

#### From Bosnia to Kosovo

Following the death of President Josip Broz Tito in 1980, the gradual disintegration of communist Yugoslavia created a power vacuum that allowed extreme nationalist movements to undermine the country's stability and social cohesion.[117] In Kosovo, the ethnic Albanian Muslim majority and the ethnic Serbian orthodox Christian minority had engaged in nationalist political struggles throughout the 1970s and 1980s. These developments facilitated the rise of Slobodan Milosevic's virulently national-ist Socialist Party of Serbia and allowed Milosevic to assume the presidency of Serbia in 1989. In the same year, Milosevic annulled Kosovo's provincial autonomy in language and educa-tion, and asserted Serbian political and cultural hegemony from Belgrade. Political divisions deepened after the collapse of the Yugoslav Communist Party in 1990 and the abrogation of the federation's one-party system. As head of the Serbian Socialist Party, Milosevic continued to rally nationalist sentiment using his control of the state media, through which he promoted the idea of a "Greater Serbia" that would incorporate the ethnic Serbian regions of other Yugoslav republics.[118]

In July 1990, Kosovo's ethnic Albanian political leaders declared independence. Serbian authorities countered this uncon-stitutional development with intensified repression in Kosovo, including the closing of Albanian-language newspapers, the renaming of Albanian streets in Serbian, and the introduction of compulsory Serbian curricula in Kosovar Albanian-majority educational institutions.[119]

The Yugoslav federation disintegrated in the early 1990s as Serbia's conflicts with Croatia, Slovenia, and Bosnia heightened ethnic tensions. The UN Protection Force in Bosnia manifestly failed to prevent the atrocities that ensued, including the mas-sacre of more than 7,000 Muslim men and boys at Srebrenica by the Bosnian Serb Army in July 1995.[120] Following the NATO aerial bombing campaign from August to September, the 1995 Dayton Peace Accords brought the Bosnian war to a conclu-sion and created two governing bodies in Bosnia. Independence eluded Kosovo, however, which was not part of the agreement, and its status remained unchanged by the accords.[121]

The failure of the United States to act to prevent mass atrocities in Rwanda in 1994 significantly affected its responses to future crises, particularly its engagement in the Balkans. On 24 March 1999, a US-led group of countries, concerned with the escalating violence directed at civilians in Kosovo, and worried that Rus-sia would block UN authorization for humanitarian intervention in the Balkans, decided to take collective action through NATO.

With the official backing of NATO, air strikes were launched against the Federal Republic of Yugoslavia. The international community had endured Milosevic's ethnic cleansing campaigns in Croatia and Bosnia throughout the 1990s, an experience that informed the decision to intervene in 1999.

The crisis in Kosovo might have been averted had the American government charged Milosevic and his counterparts with war crimes during the Dayton Accord negotiations. John Shattuck writes that peace in Bosnia "would have come sooner if the international community, led by the United States, had moved early and decisively against war criminals."[122] Shattuck argues that Milosevic's freedom from charges of war crimes gave him a "new lease" on his political life at a time when he wrongly believed that "he could afford to start another war of ethnic expulsion, this time in Kosovo."[123]

As the United States prepared for the Dayton negotiations, some wanted to harness momentum for a war crimes tribunal process. According to Shattuck, the United States was "internally divided" on the issue: the "Pentagon wanted to make sure NATO troops would not be required to hunt down and arrest war criminals."[124] Warren Christopher and US special envoy Richard Holbrooke sought the belligerents' cooperation for a tribunal, but due to congressional resistance to involvement in Bosnia they felt they did not have the authority to challenge the Pentagon on the issue.[125] Paul Heinbecker, Canada's ambassador to the United Nations, vividly recalls the media's influence on President Clinton's actions in Bosnia.[126] Heinbecker remarks that CNN's Christiane Amanpour "deserves some kind of a peace prize" because she personally had "the most direct impact on Bill Clinton."[127] Reporting from Sarajevo, Amanpour asked Clinton why he was not acting in Bosnia where thousands were dying, and the President "recoiled. He literally stepped backwards."[128] Heinbecker notes that this "was the beginning of the turn [in] the American [policy toward Bosnia]."[129]

In contrast to the Rwandan crisis, the geopolitical importance of the Balkans to the United States and its NATO allies constituted a powerful impetus for action against Milosevic. The presence of humanitarian aid groups and regional organizations in

the former Yugoslavia successfully focused international attention on the crisis.[130] Decision makers determined that a genocidal
conflagration in Europe's backyard would be an unacceptable
development for vulnerable eastern European states.

### The Racak massacre and the Rambouillet conference

Prior to the NATO intervention, the international community applied diplomatic pressure on Milosevic in the hopes of
achieving a non-military settlement. In October 1998, Richard
Holbrooke assured Milosevic that Serbia could avoid NATO
bombardment on the condition that he withdraw Serbian forces
from Kosovo and permit the entry of unarmed international
human rights observers. On 15 January 1999, Serbian forces
massacred forty Kosovar Albanians in the village of Racak,
prompting the United States to pursue coercive diplomatic
efforts. The United States threatened military force if the Serbian government did not immediately allow NATO troops into
Kosovo and demanded that Milosevic attend the Rambouillet
peace talks on 6 February. During this time, the Kosovar Albanian delegation held out for autonomy, the KLA refused to disarm,
and Serbian security forces continued to gather along Kosovo's
border while opposing the deployment of 20,000 peacekeepers.[131] Secretary of State Madeleine Albright led the efforts of
US mediators at Rambouillet to find a peaceful way to end the
dispute between the KLA and the Serbian government, but was
unable to broker an agreement on the divisive issues of Kosovo's
independence and the ethnic cleansing being conducted by Serbian forces.[132]

With warships on the Yugoslav coast and bombers on combat
alert, NATO sent a clear message that the threat of force was
not empty rhetoric. John Shattuck argues that the experience in
Bosnia set a precedent by demonstrating that the United States
was willing to use force to end mass atrocities.[133] However, this
was by no means a consensus view within the government.
Morton Halperin, special assistant to the president and senior
director for democracy at the National Security Council, comments that the Pentagon and the military "had to be dragged
into it, kicking and screaming, and would only agree if there

were no ground troops, which was an absurd way to go in."[134] Halperin asserts that the White House was not inclined to challenge the Pentagon and tried to respond "without engaging military force."[135] Furthermore, the executive branch's somewhat dubious conviction that "the American people would not tolerate more than three casualties" reflected the White House's determination to limit the potential for military engagement in humanitarian operations.[136]

Halperin contends that Madeleine Albright pressured the Clinton administration to change its view on the use of military force. "What she said to us was basically, 'None of these options that we are considering are going to stop Milosevic from driving every Albanian out of Kosovo, except the ones they kill.'"[137] Forcing out the Serbian Army became the only viable solution, "and the only way to make that happen was the threat, if necessary, to use military force against Serbia."[138]

Throughout the Rambouillet peace talks, the Serb security forces rearmed and forced 1.5 million Kosovar Albanian civilians from their homes, killing and violently attacking thousands in the process.[139] Halperin writes that a "massive buildup" of Serb military forces took place "even as Milosevic 'negotiated' at Rambouillet."[140] The pace of rearmament and the speed and thoroughness of Milosevic's ethnic cleansing led many to concur with Halperin's assessment that "this campaign of terror was planned well ahead of time. It was the cause, not the result, of NATO action."[141] The failure of the Rambouillet peace talks represented the final nail in the coffin for a diplomatic solution and led President Clinton to pursue the military option.

### UN support and NATO bombing

Although it did not authorize the NATO campaign, the United Nations indirectly supported the intervention through Security Council Resolution 1199 on 23 September 1998. This resolution described the humanitarian crisis in Kosovo as "a threat to international peace and security."[142] Although it did not encourage the enforcement of peace "through all necessary means," the resolution buttressed NATO's moral argument for intervention.[143]

On 24 October, Security Council Resolution 1203 established a Chapter VII mandate and sanctioned the Kosovo Verification Mission and the NATO Air Verification Mission, led by the Organization for Security and Co-operation in Europe, to monitor compliance with 1199.[144] However, neither resolution 1203 nor 1199 prescribed the use of force or proposed a mechanism to implement the resolutions' measures.

President Clinton viewed the air strikes as an intermediate option between doing nothing and risking the lives of American troops on the ground. In the minds of many government officials, the national interest called for action in Kosovo to an extent that had not been present in Rwanda. Deputy Secretary of State Strobe Talbott has characterized this contention as an "unpleasant but unmistakable" factor in American foreign policy.[145] While Africa is "outside the zone" of US traditional national security interests, "Kosovo, the Balkans, Yugoslavia, were inside the zone because they were European."[146] Kosovo's geographical location also meant that the political and military force of NATO could be brought to bear on the grounds of collective regional security.[147]

Michael Walzer disputes this view and has argued that US and NATO reluctance to deploy ground troops in Kosovo was a result of a lack of will to risk American lives. Walzer argues that the US Government's aversion to placing American lives in harm's way demonstrates that the national interest was not as central to the decision to employ force in Kosovo as has been widely contended.[148] In a similar vein, Edward Luttwak highlights the significance of the US decision to equip its Apache helicopters with rocket pods to suppress Serb anti-aircraft weapons, indicating that "the immediate possibility of saving thousands of Albanians from massacre and hundreds of thousands from deportation was obviously not worth [risking] the lives of a few pilots."[149]

Samantha Power, former journalist and academic, explains: "Western governments were continually engaged in the Balkans from the highest levels since 1991 in Bosnia. When Milosevic began to ramp up his crackdown [in Kosovo], there was no need to draw attention to the players in the region."[150] Ultimately, the

NATO intervention was motivated by a confluence of narrowly
perceived US national interests, moral imperative, and the desire
to demonstrate NATO's continued military prowess and prestige.

NATO adopted General Wesley Clark's plan for a ground invasion of 175,000 NATO troops after two months of lengthy internal debate. Pressure from Clark and President Clinton's national
security advisor Sandy Berger finally led to the acquiescence of
the skeptical, newly appointed US secretary of defense, William
Cohen.[151] Although ground troops were never deployed, the
agreement to deploy them marked a considerable milestone for
NATO's efforts to halt Serbia's ethnic cleansing campaign. After
intense air attacks on Serbia's power grid, Milosevic surrendered
on 3 June. NATO's reluctance to deploy ground troops and its
preference for aerial bombing diluted the effectiveness of its
campaign to halt the atrocities in Kosovo.

### The news media and public support

During the Kosovo civil war, the American news media duly
reported on atrocities committed by Serb forces. Media coverage tended to demonize Milosevic's forces, encouraging public
support for the government to "do something." As the deadline
loomed for Milosevic to accept the Rambouillet plan, the media
increasingly depicted the Serbian leader as inflexible and obstin-
ate. News reports largely portrayed the pre-war diplomatic talks
as being between a "rejectionist" Belgrade and a "reasonable and
accommodating" Washington.[152]

Media reports conveyed a sense of humanitarian urgency and
justification for the NATO intervention. On the first day of the
air offensive, 24 March 1999, *The New York Times* published
an editorial supporting the "rationale for airstrikes."[153] Yet
American news media, particularly television broadcasts, failed
to politically contextualize Serbian massacres. Stories about the
intervention led America's evening newscasts during the early
part of the offensive, but many broadcasts made no mention of
Kosovar guerillas or the civil war. In the opinion of Seth Ackerman and Jim Naureckas, the media transformed "Kosovo's civil
war into a one-sided ethnic holocaust."[154] The media coverage in

Rwanda had done the opposite, reducing the genocide in 1994 to "tribal" and "ethnic civil conflict."

American media reports on the Kosovo intervention were informed by government communiqués, which the media carried without sufficient skepticism. News agencies reported US Government denials regarding the accidental bombing of civilians.[155] Edward S. Herman and David Peterson conclude that CNN's journalists "never questioned NATO's motives, explored any hidden agendas, challenged NATO's claims of fact, or followed investigatory leads that did not conform to NATO propaganda requirements."[156] Overall, the American news media's unwitting coverage of the Kosovo crisis permitted NATO members the freedom to suggest that the intervention was the first war in history launched for purely humanitarian purposes.[157]

Several vocal civil society groups, many of which pushed for action against Milosevic, also informed the domestic debate about the intervention. Serb-American civil society groups, such as the Serbian Unity Congress, called for Milosevic's removal, and Albanian-American groups spoke out for Kosovo's autonomy.[158] These calls, combined with the news media's general support for the Kosovo intervention and simplistic reporting, narrowed the American public's debate of the issue and encouraged public support for the intervention.

### The 'g-word' debate

During the Kosovo crisis in 1999, decision makers debated the terminology of "genocide" in a manner that recalled the Rwanda killings in 1994. US War-Crimes Ambassador David Scheffer conducted a thorough study in Macedonia on whether the deportation of Kosovar Albanians constituted genocide under the Genocide Convention.[159] Scheffer's report noted that "the widespread and systematic character of the criminal conduct of Serb military, paramilitary and police units in Kosovo is among many of the indicators of genocide that we are seeing."[160]

When the NATO offensive began, the State Department approved the use of the term "genocide" to describe the campaign against Albanian Kosovars. In marked contrast to the

conflicts in Bosnia and Rwanda, the Clinton administration used
the term "genocide" in advance of intervention as a means of
garnering international public, media, and allied support.[161]

## Conclusion

The American decision-making process during the Rwandan
Genocide was deliberately riddled with political and bureaucratic obstructions to an effective response. Additionally, the
lack of domestic civil society pressure and the news media's mis-
representation of the genocide as "tribal" or "ethnic conflict"
provided no domestic impetus to respond to the genocide.

Political barriers included the formulation of PDD-25, which
constrained any US involvement in UN peacekeeping operations.
Decision makers in Washington missed several opportunities for
soft power actions such as jamming hate radio, cutting diplomatic ties, issuing stern statements of condemnation, and appeal-
ing to the media for wide-ranging coverage of the crisis. Top
decision makers instead did the opposite and instructed government officials to avoid using the term "genocide."

While some members of Congress pressured the president
to take forceful and immediate action, many senior officials in
the Clinton administration vividly recall a prevailing opinion
in Washington that Congress would oppose executive action to
stop the Rwandan Genocide. Regardless of the stance of Congress, it was ultimately the decisions of the executive that prevented American action on Rwanda. As Kenneth Roth remarks:
"You don't need an act of Congress in order to send the handful
of troops that would have been necessary to stop the Rwandan
Genocide. The buck stops at Clinton. It was his refusal to take
the political risks involved, which are ultimately the cause of
the lack of a US response."[162] Instead, the United States actively
avoided a timely and effective response to the Rwandan Genocide and pressured the Security Council to diminish the UNAMIR
mission when it was needed most.

Within the State Department, intelligence outlining the details
of the crisis in Rwanda was not widely circulated and high-
ranking officials undermined any bottom-up initiative for action

following the evacuation of Americans. Outdated Cold War strategies and narrow perceptions of the national interest continued to inform America's strategic calculations and overshadowed the long-term strategic consequences, legal responsibilities, and human considerations that ought to have shaped American foreign policy toward Rwanda. Consequently, the American response to the greatest human tragedy since the end of the Cold War was to manipulate the meaning of the word "genocide" in order to avoid coming to the aid of the Rwandan people.

There was only spotty civil society pressure on the US Government from a small number of NGOs, which sent the message to decision makers that the American public was not interested in Rwanda. To add to this, the news media misrepresented events in its limited coverage.

The Kosovo intervention illustrates that US leadership is possible when important variables converge to make the political costs of inaction unacceptable. The NATO-led intervention put an end to the commission of mass atrocities by Serbian forces and demonstrated the complexities of responding to humanitarian crises. The use of force without the official approval of the United Nations, the reliance on air strikes, the displacement of civilians in Kosovo, and the reluctance of NATO to deploy ground troops, presented significant challenges to US decision makers. However, the overwhelming need to prevent further atrocities swayed NATO partners and key decision makers to support military action.

US coercive diplomacy and NATO's credible threats of force helped avert further mass atrocities in Kosovo. The United States engaged in diplomacy, sanctions, mediation, and other non-military measures to deter Milosevic before deploying force as a last resort. After exhausting all diplomatic avenues, familiarity with Milosevic's tactics and objectives aided US decision makers in reaching their conclusion that nothing short of force would deter his aggressive and genocidal aims.

US leadership in the Kosovo crisis tipped the balance in favor of coherent international action. Having learned from past failures, the Clinton administration garnered sufficient international support to thwart Milosevic's ethnic cleansing campaign against Kosovar Albanians. Yet it is vital to note the motivation that the Clinton administration derived from the geopolitical importance of the Balkans and European stability. This demonstrates the continued influence of Cold War thinking in the United States' attitude towards humanitarian intervention. Unfortunately, this narrow conception of the national interest translated into inaction during the Rwandan Genocide and belated, but crucial, intervention in the Balkans. Despite a much higher number of civilian deaths in Rwanda, Kosovo garnered American attention because of the convergence of humanitarian and national interests.

It remains to be seen whether the preservation of innocent life from mass slaughter joined with a new understanding of the national interest will begin to shape American actions overseas. If the values codified in international treaties and conventions, many of which the United States has itself initiated and ratified, hold any meaning for US decision makers, a decisive shift towards preventing mass atrocities around the globe will emerge as a vital pillar of American foreign policy. Under these potential circumstances, plans for action will be in place the next time risks of mass atrocities present themselves and the United States will finally be able to protect its own interests while leading the world in fulfilling the promise of "never again."

## CANADA'S DECISION MAKING

### The Rwandan Genocide

By the 1990s, Canada had developed long-standing diplomatic and cultural ties with Rwanda, maintained largely through linguistic, religious, and ideological affinities among French-speaking Rwandans and French Canadians, Quebec nationalists, and the Catholic clergy in the province of Quebec. This relationship can be traced to the 1960s when members of the Québécois Catholic clergy replaced Rwanda's predominantly Belgian clergy, who had vacated the country in the post-colonial period.[163] Father Georges-Henri Lévesque, the founder and first dean of the faculty of social sciences at Université Laval in Quebec City, played a

leading role in the creation of the National University of Rwanda
in 1962, funded by Canadian development aid.[164] Recognizing
these ties, in 1992 the Université du Québec awarded Rwandan
President Juvénal Habyarimana an honorary doctorate.

The cultural links between Rwandans and Quebecers account
in part for the Canadian government's sustained development
assistance in the years following Rwanda's independence. Canadian development officials viewed Rwanda's Habyarimana
regime as more democratic than other African nations. President
Habyarimana introduced multi-party democracy and constitu-
tional reforms in 1990 after Canada and other countries tied
their aid to democratization and human rights.[165]

Despite the increasing polarization of Rwanda's political culture following the 1990 invasion by the Rwandan Patriotic Front
(RPF), a Tutsi-led rebel group, Canada exercised its diplomatic
relations with Rwanda with a view to improving human rights.
Conservative Prime Minister Brian Mulroney distinguished
himself by becoming the only Western leader to address letters
directly to President Habyarimana, pressuring the Rwandan
president to respect human rights and pursue peace negotiations
between Uganda, Rwanda, and the RPF.

When Ed Broadbent, head of the International Centre for
Human Rights and Democratic Development (ICHRDD), visited
Rwanda in November 1992 to investigate human rights violations, he was horrified by the hate speech emanating from local
radio broadcasts. Upon his return to Canada, and soon after he
initiated the International Commission of Inquiry into Human
Rights Abuses in Rwanda, Broadbent met with senior officials at
the Department of External Affairs to share his observations.[166]
The ten-person commission visited Rwanda in January 1993,
gathered testimony from Rwandan NGOs, and even dug up the
bodies of murdered Tutsis. The day after leaving Rwanda, at a
press conference in Brussels, members of the commission used
the term "genocide" to describe what they had seen. In the hope
of focusing media attention on the issue, the ICHRDD organized
a press conference in Montreal on 8 March 1993 to release the
official report of the International Commission.[167] Members of
the commission reported to the media at the press conference

that they had "uncovered evidence of war crimes and acts of genocide against the Tutsi ethnic group" and "emphasized the pervasive climate of fear and insecurity in the country," but these revelations attracted negligible interest in the media.[168]

Despite the absence of an embassy in Rwanda, CIDA officials in Kigali provided information on the security situation in 1993.[169] According to Robert Fowler, former deputy minister in the Department of National Defence, Canadian policy makers displayed an awareness and interest in Rwanda to the extent that the demands it placed on Canada's aid program frustrated some officials.[170] "There is still quite a bit of teeth-gnashing in CIDA about the amount of money that this little Rwanda got out of our Franco-African program, or indeed out of our African program," Fowler recalls.[171] "It sucked up a lot of the funds available."[172]

### An 'allergy' to African missions

In 1993, the newly-elected Liberal Government of Canada responded to a UN request to provide a force commander for a mission to Rwanda and selected Roméo Dallaire to head the observer force that later became the UNAMIR mission. However, this decision did not have the full support of politicians in Ottawa. The "Somalia affair" – involving the torture and murder of a sixteen-year-old Somali, Shidane Arone, by Canadian peacekeepers in 1993 – had poisoned official opinion against engaging in other humanitarian missions in Africa. The experience in Somalia weighed heavily on many minds in Ottawa, particularly within the leadership of the Canadian Forces.[173] "There was a certain kind of allergy to African development. In other words, we were being wrapped around the axle to such an extent in Somalia that some people had a desire to avoid African issues," recalls Kenneth Calder, former assistant deputy minister for policy at DND.[174] "It was just a kind of gut reaction. People were saying, 'When we deploy to Africa, we have problems moreso than elsewhere.'"[175] The fear that Canadians would be dragged into "something awful and ugly," without support from the Americans or other allies, presented one of the most significant obstacles to expanding Canada's humanitarian operations.[176]

There was also little interest in Africa in the highest circles of
the Government of Canada. One former External Affairs official
observes that senior decision makers in the Privy Council Office
and External Affairs remained uninvolved in Canada's Africa
policy unless absolutely necessary.[177] Similarly, Robert Fowler
recalls that at the height of the Rwandan Genocide, when decision makers were apprised of the mass slaughter, "I was amazed
and appalled to see that no one around me seemed to care a great
deal about it."[178]

Stretched for resources, the Canadian government feared
committing Canada to a mission in Rwanda that would further
strain its military capacity. The Canadian Forces were already
preoccupied with Yugoslavia, having contributed more than
2,000 troops. Louise Fréchette, then ambassador to the United
Nations, recalls that both military and civilian leaders in Ottawa
were reluctant to comply with the UN request to provide a force
commander for UNAMIR.[179] "I think the Forces considered – as
did their political masters – that we already had a lot on our
plate, and that we could not take on another big mission and
provide a significant contingent."[180] Secretary of State for External Affairs André Ouellet concurs.[181] Canada's Department of
National Defence took the position that the government had to
be "careful not to over-stretch" the Canadian Forces and that
"with all of the commitment in Bosnia, it was almost impossible
for National Defence to do more."[182]

According to Kenneth Calder, the request for a Canadian force
commander stirred up debates between DND and External Affairs
over the extent of Canada's contribution to UNAMIR.[183] Fowler,
a long-time Africanist who had a personal interest in Rwanda,
wanted to deploy Canadian troops to support Dallaire's command, but the Canadian Forces, as well as Reid Morden, the
deputy minister of external affairs, opposed the deployment.
In Morden's view, the fragile security situation in Rwanda
demanded a much larger force than Canada could provide. In an
act of compromise, the government agreed to deploy Dallaire to
UNAMIR without committing additional Canadian troops.[184]

Despite the Canadian government's awareness of the deteriorating situation in Rwanda, which had registered at many levels,

the country's political leadership and civil servants on the whole did not appreciate its significance. Incredibly, the DND briefing document that Roméo Dallaire received prior to his deployment in the fall of 1993 was only a few pages long.[185] The DND had limited intelligence on Rwanda because it was not a priority and was outside Canada's traditional zone of interest.[186] There is no evidence that the information Broadbent shared with External Affairs in 1992, which would have been critical to Dallaire's brief, was ever disseminated to DND. It is also unclear why officials at DND never contacted CIDA officials in Rwanda and Ottawa to gather more information on the country.

## Canada at the United Nations

In early 1994, signs of instability in Rwanda intensified. In January, Dallaire informed the United Nations of the presence of a Hutu extremist "shadow force." An informant, Jean-Pierre, had contacted Dallaire to warn him of weapons caches and a plot by high-level Rwandan officials to exterminate the Tutsi population and murder ten Belgian peacekeepers.[187] It is unclear how widely Dallaire's report was disseminated in Ottawa, although one External Affairs official briefed on the information from Jean-Pierre recalls that it did not seem significant: "I didn't have enough information to suspect genocide at that time."[188]

Between 6 April, when the killings began, and 21 April, when the United Nations voted to reduce UNAMIR's forces from 2,500 to 270 personnel, a consensus emerged in New York to abandon Rwanda. The Interahamwe, the extremist Hutu youth militia, had tortured and killed ten Belgian peacekeepers on 7 April, just as Dallaire's cable had warned, triggering panic in Western capitals and at the United Nations, and resulting in the evacuation of more than 100 Canadian nationals from Kigali two days later. The Department of External Affairs, in conjunction with the prime minister's office (PMO), immediately formed a task force to deal with the crisis, but it focused on the evacuation of Canadian nationals.[189]

In the wake of evidence of large-scale massacres, the UN Secretary General proposed three options to the Security Council: an immediate and massive reinforcement of UNAMIR involving a Chapter VII mandate and several thousand more troops, withdrawal of all but a small group under the force commander, or complete withdrawal. As Louise Fréchette recalls, some countries advocated a complete pullout, but Canada's position "was at least honorable. We said we did not intend to pull out and that we were open to a modification to the mandate. All we wanted was that whatever mandate is given to that force, it is commensurate with the resources it has."[190]

Canadian diplomats in New York lobbied the Security Council, UN committees, and officials to empower UNAMIR with a Chapter VII "use of force" mandate and any necessary troops, weapons, and other equipment.[191] Although Canada was not a member of the Security Council, as a troop contributor to UNAMIR it wielded some influence over the decision-making process. Fréchette recalls that, in advance of the 21 April vote, the president of the Security Council called a meeting of UNAMIR-contributing nations, at which Canada conveyed its position favoring a Chapter VII mandate and further resources for the mission.[192]

However, there is no evidence that Canada engaged in Cabinet-level discussions with Security Council members to put forward this position. Nor is there any evidence that political leaders in Ottawa directed Fréchette's lobbying activities. Fréchette appears to have acted more on Ottawa's sufferance than encouragement. According to one former External Affairs official, while the Privy Council Office (PCO) and the PMO did not oppose the position taken by the Canadian mission in New York, they did not advocate for this position.[193] If André Ouellet had a position on the future of UNAMIR during this critical period, he did not express it publicly.[194] Ottawa again demonstrated indifference toward Africa when attention to Rwanda was needed most.

Another Foreign Affairs official recalls that the position taken by the Canadian mission to the United Nations in New York was met with significant opposition, particularly from the United States. As the United States lobbied for a withdrawal, the official says, Canada found the Americans "very adamant" in their intention not to be "burned a second time after Somalia."[195] The will necessary for action was not present among Canada's most influential allies. As Maurice Baril, former head of the Military Division of the UN Department of Peacekeeping Operations in 1994, recalls, "the political will was to get the hell out of there."[196]

Despite the belief that the genocide could have been stopped during the evacuation with the deployment of just one additional brigade, the Security Council voted unanimously to withdraw all but a token force from Rwanda on 21 April.[197] The significance of the vote was not lost on those advocating a stronger mission. "I think there was a general sense of shame everywhere," Louise Fréchette observes.[198] Although the United Nations had shown itself to be unwilling to intervene despite the genocide, Canada maintained its position that any action must be carried out through the United Nations. Following the vote in May, Canada requested a special meeting of the UN Human Rights Commission in Geneva to discuss the genocide in Rwanda.

In early May, Canada adopted the United States' position that the Organization of African Unity should lead an intervention mission in Rwanda with assistance from Western nations. On 2 May, Ouellet told reporters in Ottawa that African nations were best positioned to stop the genocide.[199] On 9 May, Canadian Prime Minister Jean Chrétien discussed African intervention in Rwanda with Madeleine Albright, the American ambassador to the United Nations, who was in Canada on official business. According to a US Embassy cable, Chrétien informed Albright that Canada was prepared to commit additional troops "if necessary."[200] The cable informed the State Department that the Canadians were "focusing their efforts on the African group" at a special upcoming session of the UN Human Rights Commission in Geneva, requested by Canada to consider the situation in Rwanda.[201] This is the only evidence of discussions on Rwanda between the prime minister and the Clinton administration.

*Government knowledge of mass atrocities*

When the genocide began in April, authorities in Ottawa evacuated Canadian International Development Agency officials and other Canadian citizens from Kigali. Before the evacuation, the lead CIDA official in Kigali called a Department of External

Affairs official in Ottawa to report the massacres. "We had information early," the External Affairs official recalls, "that the young people were drunk [in the streets], that they had machetes, and were controlling the security situation. If they saw a Tutsi they would cut him into pieces."[202] Gar Pardy, the Department of External Affairs official in Ottawa who managed the Canadian evacuation in 1994, recalls no ambiguity on whether there was genocide. The only ambiguity, he says, was how the Canadian government would respond.[203]

The question of "who knew what, when" remains contested among the key Canadian actors of this period. There was a degree of situational ambiguity on the ground in Rwanda, which affected public awareness in Canada as the genocide unfolded during the critical period of 7–21 April. Many Canadian NGOs did not know enough about the genocide to communicate warnings to the government. Nancy Gordon, director of advocacy for CARE Canada in 1994, met regularly with Ouellet, his staff, and CIDA officials.[204] Although access to government was not a problem for Gordon, in meetings and conversations CARE focused on alleviating the refugee crisis. CARE's staff had left Rwanda during the evacuation and returned to work in the refugee camps across the border. CARE did not have more information than what was broadcast in the news media. "You can only communicate stuff that you have first-hand knowledge about," Gordon says. "My sense is that, in Rwanda, we didn't know. We didn't know the extent of what was happening within Rwanda itself."[205]

Some senior government officials say they did not know enough about the scale of the mass atrocities to act early, but that message is not a consistent one. Former minister of national defence David Collenette says he did not become aware of the genocide until the spread of "horrific press reports."[206] Ouellet, who was at the time focused on the troubles in Bosnia and Haiti, maintains that he did not understand the scale of the Rwandan atrocities. "In reality, there was a total lack of information about what was happening," Ouellet recalls.[207] "We didn't know. It was not something that was in the papers. Therefore, the public didn't know, and therefore, the politicians didn't talk about it or didn't look at it as an urgent priority."[208]

Although the lack of media coverage partially explains why the Canadian public was not calling on the federal government to take action, the fact that a Canadian general was in charge of the UN peacekeeping mission in Rwanda drew the attention of decision makers in Ottawa. James Bartleman, the diplomatic advisor to Prime Minister Chrétien, writes that the prime minister knew of the "tragic situation" when the genocide erupted in April 1994 and that he "followed subsequent developments."[209]

Senior politicians may not have understood the full scale of the massacres, but the government's knowledge of the violence should have compelled Ottawa to act. In an open letter to Ouellet on 19 April, the Rwandan Association of Canada publicly warned of a "large-scale massacre."[210] Despite the fact that the UN Security Council resolution of 21 April reduced UNAMIR to a small group of 270 soldiers to serve as an "intermediary" between the parties to the conflict, the resolution acknowledged "large-scale violence in Rwanda, which has resulted in the deaths of thousands of innocent civilians, including women and children."[211] As early as 11 April, the International Committee of the Red Cross had estimated that tens of thousands of people had been murdered, and on 21 April, the day of the vote, the Red Cross reported hundreds of thousands killed.[212] The Rwandan Patriotic Front had also publicly identified the atrocities as a genocide on 13 April.[213]

Evidence of the genocide had also penetrated the Parliament of Canada. Keith Martin, a Reform Party MP in 1994, recalls receiving reliable information from Médecins Sans Frontières, the Red Cross, and Oxfam. He tried to raise the issue in his party caucus meetings, as well as in Parliament, but felt that no one cared. In caucus he "brought it up many times" but "there was no interest at all to deal with this."[214] The Canadian media increased its coverage of the genocide in May, by which time Lucien Bouchard, leader of the Bloc Québécois and the Official Opposition, raised the issue in Parliament.[215] As a result, Rwanda appeared more prominently on the radar screens of senior decision makers in Ottawa. The debate in Parliament echoed in Washington on 10 May 1994, when the US Embassy in Ottawa cabled Washington to report that Bouchard had opened question period "by condemning the [Government of Canada's] 'zigzag-ging' and 'about face' on Rwanda."[216] Bouchard had criticized the government for contradicting itself on whether it would sup-port military reinforcements for UNAMIR.[217]

It is clear that the Canadian government was also bombarded with information from Kigali – unsurprising given that a Can-adian general, Roméo Dallaire, served as the UNAMIR Force Commander. Starting in November 1993, Canadian Major Brent Beardsley began sending weekly situation reports to the Directorate of Peacekeeping Operations at National Defence Headquarters in Ottawa.[218] When Rwanda's president was killed after a ground-to-air missile struck his airplane on 6 April, Major Beardsley started to communicate daily situation reports to National Defence Headquarters. Most of the reports were communicated orally. They contained much of the same infor-mation sent to the UN Department of Peacekeeping Operations (DPKO) in New York.[219] According to protocol, the Depart-ment of External Affairs would have received regular intelli-gence briefings.[220] DND held a daily Defence Executive meeting at which senior public servants and senior military personnel discussed intelligence from a wide array of sources, including NATO allies. The agenda focused on Canadian military deploy-ments overseas.[221] It is very likely that Rwanda was discussed in these meetings given the dangers that Dallaire and Beardsley faced in Kigali. It remains unclear whether intelligence on the widespread and systematic murders in Rwanda was deliber-ately buried by Canadian government officials or inadequately coordinated across departments. What is certain is that at least one key department – DND – received extensive information from Dallaire and Beardsley in Kigali and communicated with the PMO and the PCO about the crisis.

*The news media miss the story*
The news media failed to pressure Canada and the international community to increase the capacity of UNAMIR in the lead up to the 21 April Security Council vote. Media coverage underrepre-sented the magnitude of the Rwandan atrocities and misrepre-sented them as tribal warfare.[222] Where the media covered the

story in detail, it focused on the refugee crisis, not the genocide.[223] Although journalists around the world chased the story by phone from their home countries, the NGOs in Rwanda were too absorbed with saving lives to focus on taking phone calls from reporters in Ottawa or Washington. Jeff Sallot, a reporter for *The Globe and Mail*, covered the genocide from Ottawa and recalls the difficulty of trying to conduct phone interviews with people in the field.[224] It was not until he traveled to Rwanda at the end of April that he achieved a real understanding of the genocide.[225] For NGOs trying to draw attention to the genocide from the field, it was very difficult to generate media interest over the phone without photos containing "striking images" for reporters.[226]

An editorial attitude in newsrooms in Toronto and Ottawa treated Africa with the same kind of indifference displayed in the government.[227] However, a Canadian newspaper, *The Globe and Mail*, accepted an op-ed by Roger Winter, the director of the US Committee for Refugees, which was the first article to accurately describe the events in Rwanda as systematic and widespread killings – debunking the prevailing description of "tribal warfare." *The New York Times* and *The Washington Post* had rejected the piece from Winter.[228]

### Canada takes limited action

When Prime Minister Jean Chrétien learned of the escalating massacres following the death of the Rwandan president, he authorized the redeployment of two C–130 Hercules transport aircraft to support the UN peacekeeping operation in Rwanda. On the recommendation of Diplomatic Advisor James Bartleman, Chrétien ordered the planes moved from their base in northern Italy, where they served Bosnia, to Nairobi to assist the UN mission that was under the command of a Canadian general.[229] The aircraft and its forty-five member crew arrived the week of 9 April to assist in the evacuation of Canadian expatriates and other foreign nationals. Following the evacuation, the Canadian military aircraft flew regularly between Nairobi and Kigali, transporting people, goods, and supplies throughout the genocide.[230] Operating under hostile artillery and gunfire, the aircraft became what Dallaire describes as "the lifeline of my mission."[231]

Feeling pinched by a shortage of resources, DND asked Dallaire if it could redeploy one of the aircraft back to Italy to serve Bosnia, but on more than one occasion the UNAMIR Force Commander warned Ottawa and New York that, "if you cancel those Hercules, I'm pulling out."[232] At one point, Dallaire informed General Maurice Baril at the United Nations that the Canadian detachment supporting the c–130s in Nairobi had signaled that its mission was too dangerous and that it intended to withdraw. Baril immediately telephoned Louise Fréchette, Canada's ambassador to the United Nations, who responded within hours that the c–130s would not be withdrawn and would continue to serve UNAMIR.[233] Dallaire says he felt that the government provided the aircraft because a Canadian general was in charge of the UN mission, "not because of altruism by Canada."[234]

Once the UN Security Council members belatedly voted to reinforce UNAMIR with a new mandate in mid-May, Maurice Baril began contacting UN member states' diplomatic offices in New York to secure military support through the DPKO's standby force arrangement. "We were working twenty-four hours a day," Baril recollects.[235] "One night I think we sent ninety faxes requesting help ... and we were getting negative answers much faster than we ever did before."[236] Canada offered to contribute a command-and-control unit to support the new mission, called UNAMIR II, but it did not materialize because "all of a sudden we had nobody out there. The Canadians were not deploying because they had nobody to command."[237] By limiting Canada's contribution to a command-and-control unit for a mission that no one would join, Ottawa effectively bowed out of reinvigorating UNAMIR when it mattered.

Following the approval of UNAMIR II in mid-May 1994, former deputy minister of national defence Robert Fowler and deputy chief of the defence staff Larry Murray traveled to Rwanda on a fact-finding mission, primarily on Fowler's initiative.[238] Their mission was to advise the Canadian government on the supply needs of UNAMIR II. Upon his return to Ottawa in June, Fowler dispatched a powerful memorandum to National Defence Minister David Collenette, Privy Council Clerk Jocelyne Bourgon, and Chief of Defence Staff John de Chastelain, urging Canada to show international leadership on UNAMIR II and rally participating nations into action. The memo estimated that between 400,000 and one million people had been killed, and warned that Canada's reasons for inaction would be "irrelevant to the historians who chronicle the near-elimination of a tribe while the white world's accountants count and foreign policy specialists machinate."[239] Fowler described the horror of the genocide in graphic detail. In a particularly vivid passage, he recounted "the woman in Gysigny [Gisenyi] with a small baby strapped to her back methodically hacking to bits a Tutsi woman and child similarly strapped together."[240] In a damning indictment of international inaction, Fowler suggested that racist world views influenced the international failure to respond to the genocide.[241] According to Fowler, although the memo created "reverberations in the system," it failed to substantively affect policy.[242] "It simply made people feel guilty. That's all."[243]

While the international community stalled and refused to provide the reinforcements for UNAMIR II, Prime Minister Chrétien made a last-minute push for international assistance for the mission in a private meeting during the Group of 7 talks on the weekend of 9–10 July 1994. The mission was now one of humanitarian relief since Kigali had fallen to the RPF on 4 July, ending the genocide. According to Bartleman's memoir, Chrétien attempted to persuade Italian Prime Minister Silvio Berlusconi to join an intervention force but Berlusconi changed the subject. Bartleman writes that "the leaders of the seven most powerful economic countries on the planet all studiously avoided the issue during their summit."[244]

Ultimately, Canada "dragged its feet" on the deployment of UNAMIR II and did not follow through on Fowler's recommendations until the genocide had ended.[245] UNAMIR II faced such delays that the Security Council approved the French-led Opération Turquoise in its place on 22 June. Canada deployed forty soldiers on 15 July, 160 military personnel less than two weeks later, and another 160 on 16 August. Altogether, Canada contributed 450 personnel to the humanitarian mission.[246] Dallaire says that the international community delayed the deployment of UNAMIR II until the end of the genocide because leaders feared potential casualties arising from attacks by the RPF or the Rwandan government forces.[247]

Canada's limited action in the face of escalating atrocities in Rwanda in 1994 represents a policy failure. Although the response to the Kosovo crisis is not characterized as a complete success, the contrast between Canada's policies toward Rwanda and Kosovo illustrates the consequences of taking a traditional view of the national interest. MP Keith Martin notes how the narrow construction of the national interest gives rise to unfortunate and potentially disastrous perceptions. "Why Kosovo and not Rwanda? We had allies for Kosovo, we didn't have allies for Rwanda. Kosovo was seen as a European problem, with 'European' in parentheses. Rwanda was Africa – that's just what they do."[248]

### The Kosovo Crisis

#### Canada's Involvement in Yugoslavia

In 1992, the Progressive Conservative government had decided that Canada would participate in UN peacekeeping operations in Yugoslavia and, in 1993, the newly-elected Liberal government resolved to maintain Canada's international commitments in the Balkans. David Collenette, Canada's minister of National Defence from 1993 to 1996, recalls the strategic importance of Yugoslavia. "My feeling was that 'Yes, the Cold War is over but I detect signs of a revival of Russian aggression,'" Collenette says.[249] "You could see what was happening in the intelligence reports because the KGB and that whole crowd were all trying to regroup – which in effect could result in new hostilities and a new Cold War."[250]

Conflict in the former Yugoslavia was a top concern for Canada's European allies. Bill Graham, then a Liberal MP and chair of the House of Commons Foreign Affairs Committee, recalls that intervention in Kosovo became a "Canadian imperative" by virtue of European and US interests in the Balkans.[251] The intensification of the conflict in Kosovo was, according to former national defence minister Art Eggleton, "happening in NATO's backyard and it affected stability in Europe."[252] Given the length of time and peacekeeping resources NATO had devoted to stabilizing Yugoslavia, intervention was also a matter of protecting the prestige of the alliance. NATO's reputation would have suffered from a failure in Kosovo.[253]

The concern over NATO's credibility informed the drafting of the 1994 Canadian Defence White Paper, which called for a multi-purpose, combat-capable defense force, despite a CAN$1.6 billion cut to DND's budget inflicted by Cabinet between 1994 and 1998. "We were calling for new armored personnel carriers, new helicopters, submarines, but really calling for the maintenance of a combat-capable armed force, which is an armed force that is designed to fight and to kill," Collenette recalls.[254] "So I guess you could say I was a hawk."[255]

In the following years, Foreign Affairs Minister Lloyd Axworthy led the development of a foreign policy initiative based on the success of the 1997 campaign to ban anti-personnel landmines. Consequently, Canada focused its foreign policy strategy in 2000 on human security and civilian protection. The new policy prioritized the status of children in war-torn states, the legal and physical protection of civilian populations, the plight of internally displaced persons, the necessity of human rights field operations, and humanitarian intervention.[256] Critics argued that this human security policy, with its emphasis on non-military, treaty-based initiatives, was too "soft." In response, Axworthy would later characterize Canada's intervention in Kosovo as an example of human security with teeth.

In 1998, Bill Graham, chair of the House of Commons Foreign Affairs Committee, visited Macedonia. At the Kosovo border he witnessed "kilometers of line-ups of refugees trying to get across, the human tragedy of the stuff."[257] When he returned to Ottawa, he reported his observations to the governing Liberal Party caucus. "I came back to caucus and said, 'Look, this is a real human tragedy that's taking place here,'" Graham recalls.[258] "That probably had some influence on the decision that we ultimately made to participate in the NATO activities in Kosovo."[259] In contrast to the tragedy in Rwanda, Canadian parliamentarians – in this case the chair of a key committee – took a serious interest in Kosovo, travelled to the area, and called on the government to act.

*Canada and a UN mandate for intervention*

Following the failure in Somalia and the disaster in Rwanda, the Canadian Forces held the view that UN missions were poorly run, and that Canada should never again send a Canadian general into such a poorly resourced mission.[260] Graham recalls the prevailing opinion in the late 1990s that the "UN doesn't know how to run a military mission" and that they are "badly run, badly commanded, very spotty."[261] Participation in a UN mission proffered "a very good chance of a botch-up," and the forces could suffer casualties and be held responsible for the mistakes of other parties.[262] Contrarily, the Canadian military associated NATO missions with a higher probability of success, better resources, and US leadership with that country's vast military capabilities.[263]

As Canada contemplated action, David Wright, the Canadian ambassador to NATO in Brussels, communicated regularly with the minister of foreign affairs and the minister of national defence, in addition to the prime minister. In conversations and written communications, Wright reported on NATO discussions and provided recommendations, which he copied to DND, Foreign Affairs, the PMO, and the PCO.[264] Normally, Wright says, the ambassador to NATO only reported to Foreign Affairs, but the practice of reporting to the prime minister continued throughout the NATO intervention.[265]

According to David Collenette's recollection of the earlier crisis in Bosnia, Canada initially refused to support the 1995 "Operation Deliberate Force" NATO air campaign in Serbia, and only agreed to join the operation under significant pressure from the United States and other NATO allies.[266] "We had a problem convincing our own prime minister to agree to NATO bombing – he tended to be very cautious on things like that," comments Collenette.[267] "We were the holdouts. André Ouellet and I, along with officials, attended a summit in London, called by the British prime minister, John Major, to discuss the situation in Bosnia. There was tough debate and a private discussion with Major, where he really took issue with us."[268] Chrétien did not support the 1995 campaign until the Srebrenica massacre and mounting CIA intelligence about Serb massacres of Kosovars underscored its humanitarian imperatives. "We changed our position and then, I tell you, within a matter of days, NATO started bombing Belgrade, heavily. Pretty quickly, the Serbs got the message," Collenette recalls. "That's how the Dayton Accords got underway."[269]

In the summer of 1998, just three years following Operation Deliberate Force, NATO began planning for a Kosovo air campaign and other military contingencies.[270] UN Security Council Resolution 1199, passed on 23 September 1998, demanded a ceasefire between Serbian forces and the KLA, the withdrawal of Yugoslav forces, access for humanitarian aid workers, and the return of refugees and displaced persons.[271] The Americans proceeded to launch a concerted diplomatic effort to encourage European states to support NATO action, which they argued was the only way to force Milosevic to respect human rights in Kosovo. This successful lobbying effort resulted in the NATO activation order on 13 October 1998, which authorized a NATO air offensive in the event of Serbian non-compliance with Resolution 1199.[272]

By the autumn, Canadian diplomats, including Robert Fowler, then the ambassador to the United Nations, began to lobby for a UN Security Council resolution sanctioning a NATO intervention. Canada was then a member of the UN Security Council, and Fowler recalls a meeting with representatives from the United States, the United Kingdom, France, and the Netherlands, at which he made a case for securing a UN Security Council mandate to authorize NATO's use of force in Kosovo.[273] However, the three representatives at the meeting who belonged to the UN Security Council – Britain, France, and the United States – were "appalled" at the potential consequences of Fowler's proposal.[274]

NATO members expected one or more vetoes of a UN resolution; if the resolution failed, the NATO offensive would be forced to defy the will of the Security Council.[275] Such a move would, in the opinion of the United States, the United Kingdom, and France, put the credibility of the Security Council into question and "impair" their moral authority to veto future proposals from Russia or China.[276] Ottawa had given Fowler permission to argue this position at the meeting, but when it became apparent that the balance of opinion was against him by four to one, "we quickly got the message, and said, 'No, no, we won't force it.'"[277]

Once it became clear that a UN resolution authorizing a military intervention in Kosovo would not gain Security Council approval, Canada considered calling for a UN General Assembly vote to support the humanitarian intervention, but for a number of reasons decided against it. Paul Heinbecker, assistant deputy minister at the Department of Foreign Affairs, headed the Canadian government's interdepartmental Kosovo task force and reflects that one reason this initiative failed was that a General Assembly vote could not be pushed through fast enough to authorize action in the face of looming atrocities.[278] There was also concern that, because Yugoslavia was a founding member of the Non-Aligned Movement, Belgrade would leverage its membership to undermine or delay a General Assembly resolution in support of NATO action. In Heinbecker's estimation, "by the time we could have rallied the entire General Assembly to a decision that would have been useful, there would have been a lot of dead Kosovars."[279]

More importantly, the Security Council's Permanent Five strongly discouraged Canada from proposing a General Assembly vote.[280] The United States, the United Kingdom, and France again expressed concern about undermining the effectiveness of the Security Council veto. "They were all members of the veto club. None of them, not the English, not the French, not the Americans, saw this in their interests and they wanted to protect the sanctity of the veto," Heinbecker says.[281] "I have no doubt that had we been able to bring the issue to a vote in the General Assembly we would have had 150 or 160 favorable votes, maybe more."[282]

In Ottawa, Canadian officials had a short internal discussion about whether to seek a Security Council mandate for the intervention. Officials recall a debate between Fowler and Heinbecker, in which Fowler argued that NATO did not have enough political and legal authority to intervene without UN authorization.[283] Heinbecker countered that the scale of the humanitarian crisis necessitated outside intervention without advance approval by the United Nations. Canadian diplomats "chipped in their advice" as internal government cables argued one way or another over two days in February 1999.[284] The debate continued until the prime minister made his decision, at which point Heinbecker sent a message to the effect that, "the argument stops here. The policy of the Canadian government is to go into Kosovo. That's it guys."[285]

### Canada's will to intervene

Canadian decision makers generally cite the humanitarian tragedies of Rwanda and Srebrenica as informing the decision to support the Kosovo offensive in 1999.[286] David Wright recalls discussions within NATO that referred specifically to both cases.[287] According to Louise Fréchette, the UN deputy secretary general during the Kosovo crisis, Rwanda had engendered a "sense of shame" and, at least in Europe, a "hypersensitivity" toward mass atrocity crimes.[288] Art Eggleton maintains that his discussions with Major General Roméo Dallaire in the aftermath of the Rwandan Genocide affected his thinking about Kosovo.[289] "It certainly made me quite determined that if we were to ever have a situation like that arise again, we should be involved in taking action."[290] Paul Heinbecker agrees: "The world had really failed. It had failed in Srebrenica, it had failed the Rwandans in a massive way."[291]

Canadian decision makers were involved in Yugoslavia long enough prior to the Kosovo crisis that they had developed a sound understanding of the strategic importance of prevention. Canada's previous dealings with the breakup of the Yugoslav Republic had informed the opinion that, in Howard Adelman's words, "Kosovo's going to blow unless we deter Serbia."[292] Canadian decision makers believed deterrence could be accomplished through a short-term offensive.[293] After the failure of talks between Serbian leader Slobodan Milosevic and the Contact Group in Rambouillet, France in February 1999, and again in Paris in March, Milosevic's forces increased their attacks on Kosovar Albanians.[294] The debate between NATO and humanitarian NGOs regarding the effects of a bombing campaign quickly shifted from why NATO should intervene to how.[295]

In early 1999, Canada and its NATO allies began to frame military options to prevent Milosevic from undertaking an ethnic cleansing campaign in Kosovo. NATO took the stance, according to Art Eggleton, that "we couldn't allow this to continue."[296] Eggleton recalls discussions along these lines at the Foreign Affairs committee of NATO and recounts the point at which Axworthy, the prime minister, and he agreed that military intervention was necessary: "The three of us were the prime people on this file. We were of similar thought, that ... we had to have some intervention on it."[297]

"The ease with which the government made a decision on that one was quite remarkable," Calder recalls.[298] "There was nobody in Ottawa really that was opposed to the Kosovo operation. It was something which was agreed to by NATO, and all the allies agreed. People had their views of the Serbs and Kosovars, and so forth, but there was no great controversy on going in."[299]

DND questioned DFAIT over the "political endgame" of a military intervention because the military did not have any particular interest in "liberating" Kosovo.[300] That was the extent of the disagreement between DFAIT and DND, however. This discussion did not detract from DND's support for the government's decision to participate in the use of force.[301] As Fowler recalls, Foreign Affairs and DND "were absolutely *ad idem*" on the military intervention.[302]

As a member of NATO, there was little room for Canada to oppose the mission. Senior Canadian politicians acted on humanitarian principles but also wanted Canada to be seen as a reliable international ally, to strengthen alliance solidarity, and to guarantee Canada a seat at the post-conflict negotiations.[303] As the head of the government task force on the offensive, Paul Heinbecker encountered no opposition from departments or agencies and reflected that contrarians would have been "run over," in any case.[304] In a speech to the House of Commons in February 1999, Art Eggleton declared that it was "inconceivable" that "Canada would choose not to stand shoulder-to-shoulder with [its] allies."[305]

In contrast to the Rwandan Genocide, the case of Kosovo illustrates that the Canadian government was prepared to contribute
troops despite its thin defense capabilities. With eighteen foreign
missions scattered across the globe, Eggleton recalls the forces as
"stretched."[306] Chief of Defence Staff Maurice Baril and Deputy
Minister of National Defence James Judd agreed to a maximum
Canadian contribution of 1,500 troops, who would participate
in Kosovo if ordered.[307] Some Canadian military equipment
and personnel were moved to the region during the Rambouillet negotiations.[308] Canada's contribution demonstrated NATO's
resolve to use military force should diplomacy fail. Canada went
on to contribute eighteen CF–18 aircraft to the air campaign,
signifying "active participation" within the NATO alliance as
opposed to "non-opposition."[309]

### Broad-based consent

Canadian decision makers joined the intervention in Kosovo out
of humanitarian concerns and strategic interests but the government openly discussed and even publicized its humanitarian
aims. In his speech to the House of Commons in February 1999,
Art Eggleton referred to the intervention as necessary to defeat
"evil."[310] Eggleton's remark echoed his earlier warnings that
Canada must not repeat the failures in Rwanda and Bosnia.[311]

For his part, Robert Fowler says he felt that the widespread
official use of the word "genocide" in connection with Kosovo, after not using the term to describe the mass atrocities in
Rwanda, indicated that Canada's NATO allies attached greater
importance to European lives than African lives. "In retrospect,
the butcher's bill in Kosovo wasn't even a good day of the Rwandan Genocide. Not one day," Fowler contends.[312] MP Keith Martin says the contrast between the way the term "genocide" was
applied to Kosovo and not applied to Rwanda suggests that an
"institutional racism" was at play.[313]

The Government of Canada's emphasis on the humanitarian aspect of the Kosovo intervention garnered broad support
among the Canadian media. Although print media criticized the
brief time allocated for parliamentary debate over the intervention, and raised the notion that Canada was blindly following

US foreign policy, the Canadian media generally supported the Kosovo campaign.[314] In contrast to Rwanda – where the media failed to pressure the Canadian government to act – Canada and its NATO allies rallied the news media's support for the Kosovo offensive with rhetoric and communications strategies. In turn, politicians acknowledged the power of the media to rally public support for their policies. "The impact of the media is practically decisive in these things," observes Paul Heinbecker.[315] Art Eggleton notes that "the horror stories, and some of the photographs and film footage of some of the atrocities getting into the media" significantly influenced public opinion in favor of the intervention.[316] The Canadian government held a daily press briefing on the intervention, normally joined by Foreign Affairs Minister Lloyd Axworthy and National Defence Minister Art Eggleton. "This was important to counter the criticisms coming via the Yugoslav media or from critics inside Canada, especially the Serbian-Canadian community," Axworthy notes.[317]

Broad support for the mission took hold within all Canadian political parties. In Robert Fowler's opinion, "the politicians derived great comfort out of the fact of NATO solidarity."[318] The operation received cross-partisan support within the Canadian Parliament, as both the Reform Party, as the official opposition, and the Bloc Québécois, supported the intervention. Eggleton says he does not recall "any dissent whatsoever on taking action" among the major political parties.[319] On the third day of the NATO intervention, which began on 24 March 1999, New Democratic Party MP Svend Robinson supported it, arguing that his party accepted "that the use of military force as a last resort is sometimes necessary in grave humanitarian crises, when all efforts at diplomatic settlement have failed."[320]

Even in late April, parliamentary leaders hesitated to oppose the mission. The criticism of the government that did surface was generally muted or came from outside Parliament. Lawyers within Canada's Department of Foreign Affairs questioned the legality of taking action without UN approval. MP David Price questioned whether Canada had broken international law, engaging militarily without a UN mandate or declaration of war.[321] One of the most significant critics, David Orchard, a high-profile member of the Progressive Conservative Party, labeled the NATO air campaign illegal and immoral.[322] Some MPs, such as Progressive Conservative Party leader Joe Clark, charged that the prime minister consulted only with Axworthy and Eggleton in the decision-making process, to the exclusion of Parliament.[323]

Church groups and members of the Serbian diaspora led the most vociferous opposition to Canada's involvement in the NATO intervention. The Serbian diaspora in Canada held regular rallies throughout the offensive and unsuccessfully lobbied politicians, including Transport Minister David Collenette.[324] Axworthy recalls opposition from church groups concerned about the possibility of civilian casualties, but says he remained steadfast in support of the Kosovo operation.[325]

NGOs and civil society groups opposed to the humanitarian intervention risked attracting negative publicity. In reaction to the launch of the air offensive, Janet Somerville, General Secretary at the Canadian Council of Churches, told *The Globe and Mail* that, "I've been aching about this all day .... I think we are right to say, 'This is our business.' But I very much regret the decision to undertake an air war, and I do think we should be working through the UN, not NATO."[326] John Watson, CEO of CARE Canada, who personally supported the intervention, says the NGO community was divided over the legitimacy of the offensive.[327] Oxfam International did not take a position on the issue because it was too divisive for its members; Oxfam Belgium and Oxfam Canada opposed the intervention.[328] Humanitarian and human rights NGOs resisted advocating the use of force and grappled once more with a fundamental challenge that had played a part in their failure during the genocide in Rwanda.

### Conclusion

In April 2010, on an official state visit to Rwanda, Canada's Governor General Michaëlle Jean acknowledged the Canadian government's inaction during the 1994 genocide. As the first top-level Canadian official to visit Rwanda since the atrocity, she stated: "The world's failure to respond adequately to the genocide is a failure in which Canada – as part of the international community – readily acknowledges its fair share of responsibility ... It is with a sense of utmost humility that I express the respects of Canada to all Rwandans who perished, suffered, and who continue to suffer measurable loss in the Rwandan genocide."[329] Canada fell short of its responsibilities as a strong middle power and did not exploit its status as an ally of the United States, France, and the United Kingdom to lobby within the UNSC for collective action to halt the Rwandan Genocide. In the early, critical period leading up to the 21 April Security Council vote, Secretary of State Ouellet and the prime minister could have forcefully and publicly called on the United States and other members of the Security Council to support an expanded UNAMIR force with a mandate that could have halted the atrocities. To the contrary, the Canadian case study indicates that the US position to draw down UNAMIR's forces influenced the views of Canada's decision makers. As Baril remarks, "When the Americans are not implicated, or showing support for the intervention, it gives other countries the excuse not to get involved."[330] The Canadian decision to join the Kosovo intervention represented a convergence of humanitarian and traditional national interests. The experience of the Rwanda and Srebrenica genocides vested decision makers with a sense of urgency and an awareness of the speed with which civilians could become victims of mass murder. In addition to humanitarian concerns, Canada followed American and NATO leadership. Bolstered by American military resources, the Canadian military did not concern itself about equipment shortages or fears of failure that, in the view of the Canadian Forces, had characterized previous UN peacekeeping missions.

Canada's response to Rwanda also demonstrated the importance of government coordination for mounting an effective response. Decision makers regarded Rwanda, and much of Africa, with a stunning institutional indifference, which contributed to a lack of information sharing within the government about the genocide. Although officials within the Canadian government were aware of the deteriorating security situation in the Great Lakes region as early as the late 1980s, intelligence sharing on

Rwanda among DND, the Department of External Affairs, and CIDA was abysmal. Immediately following the death of Rwandan President Habyarimana on 6 April 1994, there is significant evidence that the executive branch of the Government of Canada received accurate intelligence from the killing grounds, despite claims to the contrary.

Whereas the government "stove-piped" the flow of information about Rwanda, it widely disseminated information about developments in Kosovo that led to Canada's intervention. We are unable to state definitively what intelligence was disseminated throughout the government and what high-level discussions took place about Canada's policy options in April 1994 because two key advisers to Prime Minister Chrétien, and the former prime minister himself, declined to be interviewed for the W21 Project. The Government of Canada harbors an unacceptable, pervasive culture of government secrecy that was evident in our pursuit of Canadian interview subjects and government records. It was a challenge to meet with key public officials, many of whom are now retired, for frank discussions about decisions taken fifteen years ago. Similarly, fulfilling requests under the Access to Information Act often takes a year or more. We regret that we have experienced what Canada's information commissioner, Robert Marleau, identifies as a problem relating to Canada's centralized, executive control: it grips the whole of Canadian government in a "communications stranglehold."[331]

Although the government failed to coordinate information flows about Rwanda, it streamlined the sharing of information for the Kosovo intervention. Although Canada's response to the Kosovo crisis was ad hoc, as it had been in earlier crises, the government's view of the national interest incorporated the prevention of crimes against humanity. Canada, like its NATO allies, had been involved in Yugoslavia for nearly a decade and had established strong intelligence channels providing significant information from the region. Executive power decisively determined Canada's support for the NATO operation and the prime minister became directly involved. As a result, the sharing of information across government buttressed decisive action.

The leaders we interviewed cited a shortage of civilian and military capacity as a central constraint shaping Canada's response to Rwanda. They also mentioned that Canada faced competing international crises in the Balkans and Haiti and that the Department of External Affairs suffered significant budget cuts during the 1980s. Canada did not have an embassy in Rwanda to report early warning signals of mass atrocities. But there is no evidence that Canadian officials considered using the resources that remained at their disposal. They did not consider forceful actions such as severing diplomatic relations with Rwanda or threatening to revoke thousands of Rwandan student visas, predominantly awarded to the children of the Hutu elite who were studying in Quebec.

A lack of domestic political pressure allowed Canadian officials to remain aloof toward Rwanda. As a consequence of the news media's failure in April to accurately depict the scale and political motivation behind the genocide, top Canadian decision makers felt no need to respond forcefully during the critical period before the 21 April Security Council vote. Nor did Canadian NGOs unite to lobby the Canadian government to halt the genocide.

Public support for the Kosovo intervention, on the other hand, grew out of a decision taken within the prime minister's office. The government believed that it required support from the news media, especially the dissemination of powerful images of human suffering, to sustain public support for an intervention. The role of the news media and civil society groups became critical to garnering public support for the air offensive. Reticence, as opposed to outright support or opposition, characterized the voices of NGOs regarding the intervention. Although the Serbian diaspora and some church groups opposed the bombing campaign, the majority of dissenters focused on how best to intervene as opposed to whether to intervene.

The case study of Canada's policies toward Rwanda and Kosovo illustrates the importance of building domestic political will in Canada to enable early action, especially if the United States is disinclined to show leadership. Given Canada's bilingual character, international reputation for advocating human rights, and role as an influential middle power, the country has a critical role to play in rallying like-minded nations to act. Canada must muster the will to prevent or interdict mass atrocities – particularly when such actions fall outside the traditional security or economic interests of the United States.

# PART THREE

# Policy Recommendations

Intervention is sometimes more demanding than just drop-ping food aid or sending in white UNHCR land cruisers. If the "responsibility to protect" really meant the responsibil-ity to intervene to save lives only when there is no risk of hard feelings or casualties, then the policy proposal shaped by [Lloyd] Axworthy's [ICISS] task force should have said so.

Hugh Segal, Canadian senator

## ENABLING LEADERSHIP

hortatory

The people of the United States and Canada need bold, forward-looking leadership. The president of the United States and the prime minister of Canada must take the lead on the prevention of mass atrocities. Leadership means setting clear policy priori-ties at the highest levels of the executive branch of government and sending a clear message to civil servants that preventing the abuse and slaughter of innocent civilians is one of their most important duties. Leadership needs to be enabled at all levels. This means creating a focused set of strategic preventive mea-sures and new government offices responsible for monitoring and reacting to the early warning signs of mass atrocities. Lead-ership requires the development of review processes enabling the legislative branch to hold senior government leaders accountable for acting promptly and effectively. Enabling leadership means encouraging members of the US Congress and the Canadian Par-liament to harness the voting power of their constituents to fight for genocide prevention and keeping the public informed about what the government is doing to prevent future Rwandas.

Small steps can be taken immediately to demonstrate that preventing genocide and other mass atrocities is a national priority. Although genocide occurs in the context of a complex web of factors, the United States and Canada can develop institutional mechanisms and strategies to become effective leaders in harnessing their preventive and responsive capacity to curb human rights abuses before they escalate into mass atrocities. Strong and persuasive leadership from the executive and legislative branches will reinforce the will to intervene among the wider public.

The adoption and implementation of the following recommendations will send the message that the concept of the national interest now recognizes the devastating and far-reaching consequences of mass atrocities. By making the prevention of mass atrocities a vital foreign policy objective, the United States and Canada can improve their ability to respond swiftly to protect people from the most severe forms of violence and reduce the transnational security threats that emanate from them.

### UNITED STATES

*The president of the United States should issue an Executive Order establishing the prevention of mass atrocities as a policy priority.*
The responsibility for policy change on the prevention of mass atrocities is shared by all levels of the US Government. However, each level has a unique role to play in initiating, adopting, and implementing this policy change. Efforts to institutionalize genocide prevention can only strengthen the Obama administration's goal of forging international partnerships to confront global challenges such as genocide. The president and the members of the National Security Council can prioritize foreign policy and security concerns through executive orders, which are normally used to establish a new policy, decree the cessation of an existing policy, or to attract attention to a particular issue. An executive order addressing the prevention of mass atrocities is a crucial step towards mobilizing federal government action. The president should use the State of the Union address to declare genocide

prevention a strategic security priority. The next National Security strategy document submitted to Congress by the president should incorporate genocide prevention as a core foreign policy priority and explicitly articulate this issue's connection to American national interests.

> There ought to be an executive order or presidential directive that in general terms makes it clear that it is the policy of the United States to take appropriate steps to prevent genocide. That's no more than the obligation under the Genocide Convention, but once you put it into an executive order and you've infused it into the bureaucracy, it becomes a basis for bureaucratic decision making. Then you've made a difference.
>
> John Shattuck, former assistant secretary of state for democracy, human rights and labor, State Department

*The US Congress should create a Caucus for the Prevention of Mass Atrocities.* Due to its legislative and appropriations authority, oversight by Congress is a major factor in executive branch decision making on genocide prevention. The US Congress has been a key advocate of more vigorous action on the Darfur crisis. The Darfur Peace and Accountability Act of 2005 imposed economic sanctions on oil revenues paid to the Sudanese government, required the freezing of the perpetrators' assets, and authorized aid to strengthen the African Union Mission in Sudan. In 2006, President George W. Bush followed the adoption of this legislation with an executive order imposing economic sanctions on the perpetrators of mass atrocities in Darfur.

These case-specific initiatives, while positive, have not advanced a broad policy framework for the prevention of mass atrocities. The proposed creation of a Caucus for the Prevention of Mass Atrocities would provide a forum for members of Congress to discuss common legislative objectives to address mass atrocities. The Congressional Human Rights Caucus—established to debate,

discuss, and advocate global human rights – has achieved the
elevated status of a permanent body under its new title, the Tom
Lantos Human Rights Commission. However, the all-inclusive
nature of the Tom Lantos Human Rights Commission's mandate
limits the time it can devote to preventing mass atrocities – which
certainly merit specific and sustained attention from Congress.
The creation of a Caucus for the Prevention of Mass Atrocities
would indicate Congress's commitment to genocide prevention,
demonstrate the issue's stand-alone, bipartisan importance, and
move Congress beyond rhetoric to a results-based approach to
prevention. The Caucus for the Prevention of Mass Atrocities
could liaise with the Tom Lantos Human Rights Commission to
monitor and advocate on behalf of targeted civilian populations.
The caucus could also consult with policy experts and NGOs to
assess contemporary risks of mass atrocities as reported by the
director of National Intelligence.

The Rwandan Genocide of 1994 and the mass atrocities perpetrated in Kosovo in 1999 illuminate the importance of congressional support for executive decision making. Indeed, the
executive branch often bases its plans for action on anticipated
congressional reactions. During the Rwandan Genocide in 1994,
the Clinton administration was convinced that most members
of Congress would not support an American military contribution to UNAMIR. With congressional elections scheduled for
the autumn of 1994, the executive branch was not prepared to
compromise itself politically – particularly after the deaths of
eighteen American Rangers in Somalia in October 1993.

*Members of the US Congress should take individual initiative and use their
existing powers and privileges to advocate for the implementation of the
responsibility to protect.*
Resolutions passed by the Senate or the House of Representatives do not always create law, yet they can establish a congressional position and send a message to decision makers and the
American public. Resolutions can strengthen the US Government's will to act by indicating clear congressional support for
civilian protection. The Senate has passed several "Sense of the
Senate" resolutions that have addressed the ongoing Darfur

conflict, including Senate Resolution 531 in 2005, which urged
President Bush to appoint a special presidential envoy to Sudan.
House Resolution 922, tabled by Congressman Frank Wolf in
2006, reiterated the Senate resolution. President Barack Obama
has appointed retired Major General L. Scott Gration as the
US special envoy to Sudan. House Resolution 1424, the Darfur Genocide Accountability Act, introduced by Representative
Donald Payne in 2005, set a precedent for economic sanctions
against the Sudanese government that were later adopted as part
of the Darfur Peace and Accountability Act. Other genocide-
focused resolutions include Senate Resolution 320, which sought
official recognition of the Armenian Genocide of 1915. These
calls for action signal a growing awareness within Congress that
silence on mass atrocities is no longer acceptable. Congressional
initiatives are vital to the operationalization of genocide prevention within the US Government.

The House of Representatives' power to authorize spending
gives it enormous leverage in the fight against mass atrocities.
In March 2006, the House voted to increase funding to stem the
crisis in Darfur, and in April, House Resolution 5522, the Foreign Operations Appropriations Act, provided increased funding
for foreign operations, export financing, and other related activities for the 2007 fiscal year. The late Congressman Tom Lantos,
along with his colleagues David Obey and Henry Hyde, introduced an amendment to increase humanitarian aid to Darfur by
US$50 million; the bill was adopted in 2008. Further congres-
sional support for humanitarian aid to prevent and respond to
crises in Darfur and emerging crises in other regions is urgently
needed.

In the House, we all think that we're the Secretary of State,
all 435 of us. We kind of run our own shop, to the frustra-
tion of the Administration and the State Department. We
really only answer, number one, to our districts, and to
the people in Congress. We don't necessarily listen to the
Administration. It's not like the Canadian process

where the people in power are all of the same party, and everybody for the most part is in lockstep. It's very free, it's very nice, but it's really frustrating to the Administration.

Tony Hall, former member of the US House of Representatives

Congress as a whole has supported greater funding for the State Department, new hires for USAID, and training for the diplomatic corps to enable greater preventive diplomacy in unstable regions. NGOs and think tanks have urged Congress to allocate funds to institutionalize genocide prevention within the US Government, and to build a contingency fund to respond to ongoing mass atrocities. Proposals for greater funding allocation seek to shore up the international affairs budget in the long term, and to free up funds needed for urgent crisis response in the short term. These endeavors need to be supported and pushed through in both the House and the Senate.

Holding office provides members of Congress with a unique political platform to mobilize the will to intervene. Former congressman Tony Hall, who chaired the House Select Committee on Hunger, has been dubbed the "conscience of Congress." His decision to fast to bring attention to the proposed elimination of the Committee on Hunger was taken up by students at 10,000 high schools and 200 universities across the United States. This resulted in the reinstatement of the Committee on Hunger.

Donald Payne, founder and co-chair of the Sudan caucus, was arrested for his participation in a protest outside the Sudanese Embassy in 2001, as he drew attention to the practice of slavery and genocide in Sudan. Payne's leadership brought awareness to atrocities in Sudan long before the issue was a significant one domestically. In addition to political advocacy, members of Congress must travel to increase their contact with countries at risk. Those who have traveled to witness human suffering first-hand throw a spotlight on the issue at home. There is a growing need to expand congressional action beyond Darfur to other regions.

*The US Government should foster public discussions on preventing mass atrocities.*

The Department of State and the National Security Council should create a public forum for experts, NGOs, the media, and the public to engage in a broad discussion on America's role in preventing mass atrocities. An increased level of engagement with the American people is an important objective of the Obama administration, which is convening "periodic national broadband town hall meetings to discuss foreign policy." Officials from the State Department and the National Security Council need to deploy new communications technologies to highlight the prevention of mass atrocities as a foreign policy priority.

Podcasts, webcasts, and online discussion boards can reach a broad spectrum of the American public, heighten public engagement, and improve the government's understanding of the interests, values, and concerns that Americans bring to the issue of protecting civilians abroad. Throughout the 2008 election campaign, the Democratic National Committee vigorously promoted Barack Obama's plan to "bring Americans back into their government," promising increased transparency and discussion – including the launch of twenty-first century "fireside chats." President Obama followed through on this initiative in November 2008, when he was still president-elect. It is our hope that the president will continue to use his weekly addresses to the nation to begin a national discussion of America's role in the world, emphasizing that preventing mass atrocities is vital to the American national interest and a responsibility of the US Government.

### CANADA

*The prime minister should make preventing mass atrocities a national priority for Canada.*

We believe that the prime minister has a unique opportunity to engage strategically with the US Government by establishing genocide prevention as a shared US-Canadian priority. In April 2009, US Vice-President Joe Biden identified genocide "not just as a moral imperative" but also as a "national security priority." Human rights organizations focused on the prevention of mass atrocities enthusiastically welcomed President Obama's appointment of Samantha Power, a noted journalist and genocide scholar, to the National Security Council. While President Obama has signaled his willingness to engage with Canadian-led ideas like "common security" and the responsibility to protect, the Canadian prime minister has yet to promote them in any significant way. We urge the prime minister to seize the initiative, demonstrate international leadership, and stand shoulder-to-shoulder on this issue with the US president.

We recommend that the prime minister make the prevention of mass atrocities a national priority in the next Speech from the Throne. Each year the Canadian Parliament marks its return from the summer recess with the governor general's throne speech detailing the prime minister's policy priorities for the upcoming year. In the 2007 throne speech, Prime Minister Stephen Harper committed his government to increasing trade with Latin America, advancing economic development and public security in Haiti, and maintaining Canadian troops in Afghanistan until 2011. In the 2008 Speech from the Throne, the prime minister named supporting democracy as a foreign policy priority, declaring: "Security ultimately depends upon a respect for freedom, democracy, human rights and the rule of law. Where these values are imperiled, the safety and prosperity of all nations are imperiled. Canada must have the capacity and willingness to stand for what is right, and to contribute to a better and safer world." To advance this goal, the prime minister proposed strengthening the Canadian Forces and creating a program for international development assistance that more explicitly links aid to the promotion of democratic governance.

While these priorities provide a solid foundation for Canadian leadership on the issue of prevention, it is imperative that the government dedicate greater attention to preventing mass atrocities wherever feasible rather than confining its attention to a few areas. Indeed, limiting the government's focus reduces its ability to monitor global threats as they arise. Resources must be assigned to construct appropriate long-term strategies to prevent mass atrocities, using Canada's foreign aid, diplomacy, and military capabilities. By focusing on a broad, pro-active approach to monitoring and acting on escalating crises, the government would advance the priorities outlined in its 2007 and 2008 throne speeches.

We recommend that the prime minister use the Speech from the Throne to recognize the intersection of Canada's national interest with the prevention of mass atrocities and pledge to work with allies to protect civilians around the world from mass murder. In tandem with the throne speech commitment, the prime minister should announce the formulation of a new policy statement on the prevention of mass atrocities, outline the rationale for the policy, and set a deadline for its final adoption by Cabinet. The prime minister must articulate the importance of phasing out reliance on reactive measures and highlight the need for speedier action and improved coordination throughout government to implement the new proactive policy. To ensure effective results, the Cabinet should appoint a senior interdepartmental coordinator to direct the policy statement consultations and formulation.

A throne speech announcement and the development of a national prevention policy require a minimal expenditure of political capital by the prime minister but would reap significant rewards. By implementing this recommendation, the prime minister would engage the Canadian electorate on an issue of vital importance. The pragmatic and moral appeal of combating mass atrocities has the potential to garner unifying support across Canada's political, regional, ideological, and religious divides. By making the prevention of mass atrocities a national priority, the government would encourage NGOs, think tanks, and academics to work with the government to devise creative and effective policy solutions.

*The prime minister should appoint an international security minister as a senior member of the Cabinet.*
As our study on the Canadian response to the 1994 Rwandan Genocide demonstrates, ad hoc and ineffectual responses to mass atrocities are often attributed to confusion over the appropriate

channels for action within government. When mandates are not clearly articulated – particularly within the public service – no one will assume ownership and take responsibility when it is required. Gareth Evans makes the point well: "If everyone is responsible then no one is responsible."

The prime minister needs to demonstrate strong leadership on the prevention of mass atrocities by creating a new Cabinet-level position, the minister of international security, who exercises leadership on the prevention of mass atrocities. As a senior minister with the gravitas and experience to forge a coherent policy between the different levels of government and across departments, the international security minister would coordinate defence, diplomacy, and development policy. In addition, the mandate of this portfolio would include surmounting the key institutional challenges within the government on preventing mass atrocities and issuing early warnings based on information drawn from relevant departments and agencies. There are two main reasons why the appointment of the international security minister would be an important step. First, a cabinet minister normally operates beyond the confines of interdepartmental "turf wars," which would boost the efficiency of formulating prevention policy. A senior cabinet minister armed with a mandate from the prime minister could punch through the hierarchy of governmental bureaucracy when necessary. Second, the international security minister would serve as the high-level official responsible for prevention policy.

International security policy is the link between foreign policy and defence policy. There are, however, major political and institutional challenges to coordinating diplomatic, defence, and development policy. This is why the proposed international security minister must be a senior figure within Cabinet who operates with the confidence of the prime minister and is armed with a mandate to influence policy options and broker agreements between departments and agencies, particularly the Department of Foreign Affairs and the Department of National Defence. The government's Afghanistan Task Force shows what an influential cabinet minister can do. Although a deputy minister based in the Privy Council Office heads the task force, the Cabinet Committee

on Afghanistan manages it. This management structure is effective because an influential cabinet minister chairs the Cabinet
committee and has the authority to act decisively in close consultation with the prime minister. The international security minister would present memoranda to Cabinet relevant to genocide
prevention, meet with other ministers and senior-level civil servants from relevant departments and agencies, monitor emerging or ongoing crises, and brief the prime minister, members of
Cabinet, and parliamentary committees on a regular basis.

*The Government of Canada should support and promote public discussion
on Canada's role in preventing mass atrocities.*
The Department of Foreign Affairs and International Trade has
hosted online discussions, which provide opportunities for NGOs,
academics, students, and citizens to offer their points of view.
Since 2003, Foreign Affairs has used these discussions to gauge
the opinions of Canadians on Canadian sovereignty, nuclear and
small arms non-proliferation, the global economy, participation
in multilateral institutions, and other issues. DFAIT has followed
up these discussions by summarizing them and posting responses
for public review.

The Government of Canada would benefit from a national
discussion on Canada's role in preventing mass atrocities. Both
Liberal and Conservative governments have recognized the
importance of these national dialogues – the National Forum on
Foreign Policy and the Foreign Policy Dialogue are two important examples. The National Forum hosted public discussions
across Canada and provided online questionnaires about policy
debates, while the Foreign Policy Dialogue measured Canadian
public opinion on foreign policy goals after 9/11.

At a time when Canada's role in the world is being debated,
it is important that the Canadian government open its foreign policy to online public comment and arrange for a series
of public town halls and community dialogues. These public
forums should probe the broad question of what should constitute the Canadian national interest, and include a discussion on Canada's role in the prevention of mass atrocities. The
initiative would allow the government to explore the public's

understanding of Canada's national interest in a more intercon-
nected, globalized world.

The Government of Canada should inform the public that the
rise in intrastate conflict and the targeting of civilians requires
changes in Canada's traditional role as a peacekeeping nation.
The complexity of intrastate conflict, and the willingness of
some state powers to repress segments of their own populations,
ultimately threaten global security – a pillar of Canada's national
interest – and cry out for a reassessment of the status quo.

*The Parliament of Canada should convert the All-Party Parliamentary Group
for the Prevention of Genocide and Other Crimes Against Humanity into a
standing joint committee.*

Parliamentarians can play a crucial role in the prevention of
mass atrocities. The importance of parliamentary leadership cannot be overstated. As national leaders in Ottawa, they carry out
the key responsibilities of representing Canadians and holding
the government accountable. Their work in Canada's legislature
has brought national attention to crimes against humanity and
has led to concrete government action.

Parliamentary committees provide an important platform
for members of Parliament and senators to operationalize the
responsibility to protect. At present, the issue of preventing mass
atrocities falls within the remit of several parliamentary committees, which has led to a fragmentation of efforts. For example,
the House of Commons Committee on Foreign Affairs and International Development, and the Senate National Security and
Defence Committee study and discuss issues related to genocide
prevention. In addition, the House of Commons Subcommittee
on International Human Rights engages in important work on
mass atrocities and in early 2009 held hearings on the troubling
human rights violations suffered by the Bahá'í community in
Iran. For all their good work, not one of these permanent committees has an exclusive mandate to study the global destabilizing threats of mass atrocities.

The All-Party Parliamentary Group for the Prevention of
Genocide and Other Crimes Against Humanity provides a locus
for members of Parliament and senators to hold non-partisan

discussions on this important issue. The all-party group, founded by Senator Roméo Dallaire, is self-mandated to ensure that the Canadian government does all it can to prevent mass atrocities, but it does not have the status, privileges, or authority of a regular parliamentary committee. This means that it has no legal power to summon government officials or expert witnesses, does not have a budget for staff and travel, and lacks the authority to table committee reports.

In order to encourage responsibility and enable leadership within Parliament, we recommend that the Canadian Parliament convert the All-Party Parliamentary Group for the Prevention of Genocide into a standing joint committee composed of senators and members of Parliament. This crucial step will give the all-party group the necessary power and resources to effect change on a national level. Although standing joint committees are rare, there is a precedent for this kind of arrangement. The Standing Joint Committee on the Library of Parliament and the Standing Joint Committee for the Scrutiny of Regulations are comprised of members of Parliament and senators.

In November 2005, Bill C–81 was introduced in the House of Commons to create a standing joint committee called the National Security Committee of Parliamentarians; it proposed that the committee receive all the necessary powers of a regular parliamentary committee. Under similar terms, Parliament should create a new standing joint committee with the authority to call upon Cabinet ministers and senior officials to testify and the resources necessary to bring Canadian and international experts to Parliament Hill to brief parliamentarians. The committee could conduct hearings on Canada's civilian and military capacity to prevent mass atrocities. Furthermore, it could formulate regular reports on Canada's anti-genocide strategies and monitor the government's steps to implement the responsibility to protect. Reports could be tabled in Parliament advocating increased funding for departments aimed at building preventive capacity. The committee could pass motions calling for preventive or responsive action and refer them to Parliament; it would provide a much-needed forum for civil society organizations, government officials, and parliamentarians to explore how to improve Canada's foreign policies in the sphere of prevention. This new committee would give parliamentarians a permanent mechanism to discuss and advocate a made-in-Canada anti-genocide agenda.

*Parliamentarians should exercise individual initiative and use their existing powers and privileges to advocate the implementation of the responsibility to protect as an international norm and a vital part of canada's foreign policy.* The parliamentary system allocates significant power and responsibility to members of Parliament and senators, but currently there is no substantial national discussion on the responsibility to protect. Parliamentary debate, particularly during Question Period, provides an important opportunity for raising the visibility of R2P. Members of Parliament and senators can actively promote and advocate the prevention of mass atrocities by individually tabling legislation and motions.

Some MPs have demonstrated the individual initiative necessary to bring these issues to the attention of the House of Commons and the government, but much more needs to be done. MP Keith Martin has utilized question period to call on the government to operationalize key aspects of the responsibility to protect. In April 2007, he asked the government to expel Zimbabwe's top diplomatic representative to Canada on the grounds of Zimbabwe's egregious human rights violations. However, more than a few questions in Parliament are necessary to engender lasting and effective change.

Tabling motions in Parliament can be an effective way of drawing attention to the responsibility to protect. According to the rules of Parliament, these motions must be debated, generating national discussion of the issue. If a motion passes, it can have a significant impact on building political momentum for action by the government. For example, on 8 May 2007, the Senate passed Senator Hugh Segal's motion to recall the Canadian ambassador from Zimbabwe and sever all diplomatic ties with the country. In another case in 2008, the House of Commons unanimously agreed to MP Irwin Cotler's motion, designating 7 April, the start of the Rwandan Genocide, as an annual "Day of Reflection on the Prevention of Genocide." Similarly, on the initiative of Senator Shirley Maheu, the Senate of Canada passed a motion in 2002 that officially recognized the Armenian Genocide, which laid the foundation for the House of Commons to recognize the genocide with a similar motion in 2004, against the wishes of the Liberal government. In 2006, the Conservative government recognized the House and Senate resolutions commemorating the Armenian Genocide.

Individual members of Parliament and senators should use their power to introduce private members' bills to bring attention to issues. MP Irwin Cotler, who tabled Bill C–536, the Sudan Accountability Act, in April 2008, showed what can be done. The bill proposed important soft power actions, namely economic divestment by the Canadian government from any Sudanese business operations and investments. The legislation did not pass into law, but it brought the mass atrocities in Darfur to the attention of the Canadian government, the media, and the public.

## ENHANCING COORDINATION

During the course of our research, numerous experts expressed concern that there are no established governmental processes or mechanisms in Washington or Ottawa designed for preventing and responding to mass atrocities. A first requirement for achieving this end is the improvement of government coordination within the American and Canadian governments. Coordination involves the flow of intelligence across government departments and agencies and the ability of key decision makers to act decisively on this information in a concerted, timely, and coherent manner. Overcoming competing institutional interests and cultures requires enhancing interdepartmental and interagency exchanges and exploiting the diverse competencies of each arm of government. Every relevant government agency and department should be authorized to draw upon its human and material assets to bring a broad range of perspectives and options to the discussion table.

Establishing permanent, interdepartmental, and interagency bodies designed explicitly to prevent mass atrocities would encourage civil servants to channel intelligence to key decision makers and permit the identification of who is responsible for decisions. These measures would also benefit NGOs and advocacy groups looking for access points when they need to submit representations aimed at preventing or stopping mass atrocities.

## UNITED STATES

*The president should create an Atrocities Prevention Committee to coordinate interagency policy on the prevention of mass atrocities.*
The Genocide Prevention Task Force, co-chaired by Madeleine K. Albright and William S. Cohen, released its policy report, *Preventing Genocide: A Blueprint for U.S. Policymakers*, in December 2008. Based upon sector-specific consultations with American policy experts, the task force formulated specific recommendations that aim to institutionalize genocide prevention at all levels of the US Government. One of the primary problems revealed by the Genocide Prevention Task Force and the W21 Project is the shortage of effective interdepartmental coordination. Based on our findings, W21 strongly endorses the task force's recommendation for the creation of an Atrocities Prevention Committee.

Although the Office of the Coordinator for Reconstruction and Stabilization, a permanent interagency office within the State Department, currently coordinates peace building initiatives, an equivalent body dedicated to the prevention of mass atrocities does not exist. An Atrocities Prevention Committee (APC) would provide a permanent body for interagency contact and coordination for the prevention of mass atrocities. Led by the White House, the APC would be co-chaired by officials from the National Security Council and the State Department and would include representatives from the departments of Defense, Justice, Treasury, and USAID. The APC would be responsible for reviewing country situations where mass atrocities may be likely, producing risk and early warning assessments, and developing prevention and response strategies. The committee would regularly brief members of Congress and receive briefings from the director of National Intelligence. The creation of the APC would initiate the long-term process of institutionalizing prevention policy and in the short-term would provide a focal point for the coordination of prevention and response actions.

During the Rwandan Genocide in 1994, an ad hoc Interagency Working Group was created to coordinate the evacuation of Americans from Kigali. Following the evacuation from Rwanda, and under the leadership of the State Department, this working group sought to sustain UNAMIR. However, the working group's authority was overridden by the NSC-led Peacekeeping Core Group's decision to withdraw UNAMIR. Due to resistance from powerful individuals in the National Security Council who gave low priority to halting mass atrocities, the working group was unable to mobilize the government to take action. In the interest of preventing these bureaucratic blockages, the Atrocities Prevention Committee should be co-chaired by a senior official from the National Security Council and an assistant secretary from the State Department. Furthermore, the mandate of the State Department's assistant secretary for democracy, human rights, and labor should be expanded to include genocide prevention. This broader mandate would permit the assistant secretary to serve as a designated point of interagency contact within the State Department and advocate within government for prevention policy and responsive actions.

*The national security advisor should create an Interagency Policy Committee on Preventing Mass Atrocities to coordinate policy across the executive branch and liaise with the Atrocities Prevention Committee.*
Interagency Policy Committees (IPCs) have become a key feature of decision making within the US Government. President Barack Obama's first Presidential Policy Directive, PPD–1, outlined the composition of his National Security Council and proposed significant steps to facilitate interagency coordination. PPD–1 instituted IPCs mandated to manage, implement, and coordinate horizontal national security policies. The directive also expanded the National Security Council to include the attorney general, secretary of the treasury, secretary for homeland security, US ambassador to the United Nations, and the president's chief of staff, as well as other political aides. The directive invites cabinet

members to attend every session of the National Security Council. With this directive, President Obama has created a more inclusive decision-making body at the executive level and introduced a more coordinated approach to policy making.

There is a growing need for a specialized Interagency Policy Committee on Preventing Mass Atrocities that can coordinate policy development and implementation at the executive level. The Interagency Policy Committee on Preventing Mass Atrocities would hold meetings convened by the National Security Council. These meetings would include White House political aides, the secretary of state, secretary of defense, secretary of the treasury, secretary of justice, and the administrator of USAID, as well as the deputy assistant secretaries from relevant government agencies. The Interagency Policy Committee on Preventing Mass Atrocities, informed by reports and insight from the Atrocities Prevention Committee, would discuss US policy options toward countries at high risk.

An IPC on Preventing Mass Atrocities would inspire a move away from reactive policies. In order to shift the emphasis to prevention, it is imperative that the US Government institutionalize a monthly interdepartmental review of US policy toward countries at risk of mass atrocities. This review needs to investigate the effectiveness of US policy across the State Department, National Security Council, Department of Defense, Department of the Treasury, Department of Justice, and USAID. The policy of the United States toward crisis regions and international peace support operations would be reassessed at the executive level. Under the leadership of the national security advisor, the committee would evaluate policy reviews conducted by the APC to determine whether US policy corresponds to realities on the ground.

The establishment of an IPC for the Prevention of Mass Atrocities would directly address some of the US Government's coordination failures during the Rwandan Genocide. The United States did not respond to Rwanda's escalating violence in 1994 partly due to a restrictive peacekeeping policy, embodied in Presidential Decision Directive–25, which deliberately limited American involvement in UN peacekeeping operations following the debacle in Somalia. This policy, which became official a month after the genocide began and two weeks after the United States voted for a UN withdrawal from Rwanda, obviated consideration of US action in Rwanda. Senior decision makers held the view that the president did not want deliberations on further peacekeeping missions, explaining why the National Security Council did not hold any principals' meetings on Rwanda. An IPC for the Prevention of Mass Atrocities would close this gap by requiring decisions from the expanded National Security Council, which now includes committee participation from the president's advisors and the US ambassador to the United Nations.

*The national security advisor should create standard operating procedures for disseminating intelligence on the risks of genocide and other mass atrocities.*

The national security advisor should outline clear standard operating procedures for disseminating intelligence on threats of mass atrocities. Intelligence analysis has to reach all relevant branches of government, including the president, cabinet members, and appropriate Department of State bureaus. Warnings of these threats need to be circulated to all members of the APC and the IPC on Preventing Mass Atrocities. Better coordination of information flows within the US Government can address some of the problems identified in the W21 case studies of Rwanda and Kosovo and ensure that all relevant decision makers have access to the same information. A transparent mechanism for information sharing also improves accountability.

While critics devote considerable attention to the need for improved early warning capacity, the case studies of Rwanda and Kosovo illustrate that the government should place greater emphasis on improving internal analysis and the sharing and channeling of information. During the Rwandan Genocide, Washington received unambiguous intelligence reports of escalating violence and evidence of plans for the targeted slaughter of civilians. The W21 Project has determined that inadequate standard operating procedures on the flow of intelligence, compounded by a lack of in-depth analysis on the risks of genocide, contributed to the government's failure to build and coordinate an effective response in 1994. In contrast, the United States' long-term presence in the Balkans gave it first-hand knowledge of the region's history, politics, and risks of deadly violence under the direction of Serbian leader Slobodan Milosevic. The government's early coordination on Kosovo – drawing on intelligence from many departments and agencies – impacted directly on US action to prevent further mass atrocities in Yugoslavia.

### CANADA

*The Government of Canada should create an interdepartmental Coordinating Office for the Prevention of Mass Atrocities.*

Four years after the Canadian government affirmed its commitment to R2P at the 2005 World Summit, there is no interdepartmental body to lead and coordinate prevention policy. To advance the objectives outlined in the 2005 World Summit Outcome document, we recommend that the Canadian government create a Coordinating Office for the Prevention of Mass Atrocities to coordinate action. The Coordinating Office should receive a focused mandate from the Cabinet and fall under the responsibility of the proposed international security minister.

The Government of Canada customarily establishes temporary interdepartmental coordinating committees, or task forces, comprised of deputy ministers and other senior civil servants, in response to overseas crises. Interdepartmental task forces were established for the 1996 eastern Zaire crisis and the 1999 Kosovo crisis. Although temporary task forces can provide stop-gap responses, the continuation of ad hoc reactions to these crises is symptomatic of the government's failure to recognize mass atrocity crimes as a recurring global problem. The government must establish a permanent body fully equipped to handle prevention and response.

Some steps have been taken toward a more holistic, coordinated approach. In 2005, the Department of Foreign Affairs established the Stabilization and Reconstruction Task Force (START) to coordinate government policy on international security and stabilization. However, START's mandate says very little about the prevention of mass atrocities. Furthermore, only one mid-level official within the department works full time on the responsibility to protect and that individual is situated outside of START. Several experts consulted for the W21 Project were unsure of START's coordinating authority and whether it would be an effective mechanism to operationalize R2P. Given START's broad mandate – which includes responding to natural disasters and coordinating peace building initiatives – a new interdepartmental office, with an exclusive mandate to prevent mass atrocities, is essential.

The proposed Coordinating Office would provide a permanent point of interdepartmental contact for the prevention of genocide. The office would have the authority to convene regular interdepartmental meetings, which would include officials from the Department of Foreign Affairs, Department of National Defence, Privy Council Office, Canadian International Development Agency, Department of Public Safety, Canadian Security Intelligence Service, and the Department of Finance, as well as any other agencies whose relevance is clear. Meetings would serve as forums to discuss prevention and response strategies and assess whether Canada's policies toward countries at risk are consistent with shifting realities on the ground. The Coordinating Office would also play a key role in briefing the international security minister and parliamentary committees.

The Coordinating Office for the Prevention of Mass Atrocities would also serve as a permanent interdepartmental body within the Canadian government to lead the analysis of threats of mass atrocities. It is necessary that the office be supported by a Cabinet decision that initiates government-wide programs and policies for the prevention of mass atrocities. This critical step would demonstrate the prime minister's commitment to building a long-term prevention strategy. With a mandate from Cabinet, the Coordinating Office would coordinate a whole-of-government framework to analyze risks of mass atrocities. The office would work with senior managers in the public service to ensure that effective prevention policies, resources, and leadership on the responsibility to protect pervade all relevant departments and divisions.

The failure to coordinate and adequately share intelligence within the Canadian government partly contributed to its failure to act early in the Rwandan Genocide. Indeed, several individuals in the Canadian government were aware of the deteriorating security situation in Rwanda long before the genocide erupted in April 1994. However, there is no evidence that these warnings were widely circulated across departments, nor was there a process for sharing them with Roméo Dallaire prior to his deployment as Force Commander to UNAMIR in 1993.

> I think we have to use the resources that we have more effectively. Between CIDA, Defence, and Foreign Affairs, we need to look at how we can more deeply integrate those departments. We need to have a whole approach that looks at all those resources and says, "Well, how can we actually get more out of this than we're getting?" Frankly, it's advice not only for ministers, but advice for the country.
>
> Bob Rae, Canadian member of Parliament

The Government of Canada has learned from previous experiences. The 1999 Kosovo intervention was conducted in almost complete contrast to the Canadian government's failed response in Rwanda. Rapid and decisive government action was possible due to the prime minister's creation of the Kosovo Task Force, mandated to share information and coordinate action across government departments. A newly created Coordinating Office for the Prevention of Mass Atrocities would receive a substantive mandate directly from the prime minister and Cabinet and have the authority to lead Canada's policy implementation of the responsibility to protect.

*The Coordinating Office for the Prevention of Mass Atrocities should create standard operating procedures for disseminating intelligence concerning the risks of mass atrocities throughout the whole of government.*

It is essential that the Coordinating Office for the Prevention of Mass Atrocities create and implement standard operating procedures to ensure that intelligence pertinent to the threat of mass atrocities is communicated vertically and horizontally within government. It is necessary that risk assessment reports swiftly reach key decision makers, including the prime minister, the proposed international security minister, minister of national defence, minister of foreign affairs, minister of international cooperation, and other relevant senior officials. Standard operating procedures would dictate regular reviews of Canadian policies towards high-risk areas of the globe and ensure that decision makers have access to the information necessary for preventive policy actions.

The failure to share information during the Rwandan Genocide underlines the vital need to establish mechanisms that ensure critical information about potential mass atrocities is immediately delivered to the highest levels of government. Throughout the Rwandan Genocide, the Canadian contingent stationed with UNAMIR in Rwanda communicated daily situation reports to National Defence Headquarters in Ottawa. However, it is unclear how widely this information was circulated within government. Although Prime Minister Jean Chrétien was informed of the massacres in early April, Minister of National Defence David Collenette and Secretary of State for External Affairs André Ouellet told us that they were not aware of the scale of the violence in Rwanda until the media reported it in earnest. It is unacceptable that critical intelligence on mass atrocities is not automatically shared with ministers. There must be clearly defined, obligatory procedures to inform the prime minister and relevant members of the Cabinet so that the departments can be mobilized into action.

## BUILDING CAPACITY

A state's capacity for the prevention of mass atrocities is comprised of its civilian and military capabilities. A shortage of either civilian or military capacity diminishes the political will for action. Civilian capacity consists of non-military measures available to a government to encourage positive state behavior through diplomacy, economic incentives, or other inducements. Civilian capacity can also thwart negative state behavior through

punitive measures such as travel and study bans, economic sanctions, and the severing of diplomatic ties. However, military
capacity is also essential. It enables decision makers to reinforce
soft power options with credible threats of hard power actions.
In the absence of civilian capacity, governments are only left with
two options: doing nothing or applying force hastily. A state pos-
sessing soft power has the credibility, legitimacy, and influence
to affect international situations without having to resort to the
use of force.

> The sad fact is that the US Government and the UN are only
> able to respond to two to three crises at one given time.
>
> Andrew Natsios, former administrator of USAID

A majority of the experts we consulted singled out overburdened civilian and military capacity as a significant obstacle to
American and Canadian leadership on the responsibility to protect. The ongoing military operations in Iraq and Afghanistan
have depleted much of Canada and the United States' defense,
diplomatic, and development resources, vastly diminishing the
political will to engage in humanitarian intervention as defined
by R2P.

It is shortsighted and ultimately dangerous for the United
States and Canada to overlook the pressing need for a permanent policy for the prevention of mass atrocities. Robust civilian
and military capacities – which would equip them with the necessary resources to prevent mass atrocities and face the pressing
global challenges of the twenty-first century – are essential to the
long-term interests of the United States and Canada.

> I think there are two different struggles here, and they are
> both very important. One is the creation of the instru-
> ments. All this rhetoric, in my view, is irrelevant if we don't

have these peacekeeping forces, we don't have these civilian intervention forces, and we don't have the capacity
to understand and deal with conflicts and help mediate
them... The other is to continue to work on the definition,
that it is in the American interest to promote the doctrine
of the responsibility to protect and to try to expand it,
deepen its roots in society.

> Morton Halperin, former special assistant to the president
> and senior director for democracy at the National Security
> Council

## UNITED STATES

*The US Government should allocate federal funding to institutionalize the*
*prevention of mass atrocities within civilian agencies.*
The US Government currently focuses primarily on conflict
response, stabilization, and reconstruction but does not prioritize preventive measures for mass atrocities and genocide. In the
existing US Government organizational framework, the Office
of the Coordinator for Reconstruction and Stabilization, located
in the State Department, is tasked with fostering political stability internationally. While stabilizing political structures is a
desirable goal, the mandate of the Office of the Coordinator for
Reconstruction and Stabilization, its Civilian Response Corps,
and USAID's Office of Transition Initiatives, should be revised to
include the prevention of genocide and broader mass atrocities
in their frameworks for action.

Despite a budget of roughly US$150 million per year since
2006, and additional transfer payments from the Department
of Defense of US$100 million for the Office of the Coordinator
for Reconstruction and Stabilization to support its peacebuilding
and reconstruction activities, no funding is provided for monitoring and preventing mass atrocities within this interagency
office. New funding should be allocated to USAID, the Department of Defense, and the Department of State for the purpose

of institutionalizing genocide prevention. Allocating funds to prevent mass atrocities will cost less than reactive measures. A portion of government funding ought to be allocated to the proposed activities of the Atrocities Prevention Committee.

*The US Government should re-establish its soft power capacity by expanding its diplomatic and development corps and enhancing the field training of USAID and State Department officials.*
The ability of the United States to achieve its foreign policy priorities abroad depends upon the legitimacy of its international reputation and the appeal of its foreign policy, political culture, and engagement with the international community. Winning the "hearts and minds" of foreign populations during key historical moments – such as the Second World War and the Cold War – was partly achieved through the appeal of America's culture, political values, and diplomatic influence. The United States acquired "soft power," defined by political scientist Joseph S. Nye as the ability to make others want what you want without any explicit exchange or threat taking place. America's capacity for soft power has dwindled over the years and is in need of reinvigoration. The Center for Strategic and International Studies, a public policy think-tank in Washington DC, has highlighted the erosion of American soft power and proposed a Smart Power Initiative to help the United States engage more deeply with the rest of the world and re-establish its internationalist reputation.

Soft power capacity must be enhanced within USAID and the State Department by expanding the number of deployable personnel and improving their training. USAID had a permanent staff of 15,000 in the late 1960s, but by 2009 that number had dwindled to 3,000. Operations in Afghanistan and Iraq have consumed State Department consular staffing; currently one quarter of US foreign embassy posts are vacant. According to a report issued in 2008 by the Friends Committee on National Legislation, ninety-four per cent of the US budget for international affairs is allocated to military spending, while only six per cent is allocated to diplomacy, early warning, and peace building. The erosion of the diplomatic and development corps reduces the US capacity to prevent future mass atrocities. Unless this trend is reversed, the United States will be obliged to use military options more frequently. Addressing this deficiency requires increased funding for new hires. Foreign Service officers with country-specific skills such as knowledge of foreign languages, cultures, histories, and politics, as well as the broader skills of diplomacy and negotiation, need to become the standard for the US diplomatic corps.

Former secretary of state Condoleezza Rice first proposed the expansion of the foreign service in 2006 to enable "transformational diplomacy" aimed at the multilateral promotion of stable and responsible states. The proposal's laudable goals included doubling the number of deployable Foreign Service officers over a ten-year period, but funding for this important initiative has yet to materialize. The Obama administration has called for reinforcing US diplomacy and the National Security Council has advocated expanding America's overseas diplomatic presence as a pillar of US foreign policy. Moreover, it has pledged to "stop shuttering consulates and start opening them in difficult corners of the world – particularly in Africa [and] expand our foreign service, and develop our civilian capacity to work alongside the military." It is necessary that these calls for more funding and personnel be implemented to improve America's preventive capabilities.

*The Department of Defense should develop and incorporate doctrine and rules of engagement for preventing and responding to mass atrocities and train the US military in civilian protection.*

The US military is a key component of the American government's capacity to prevent mass atrocities. As a prerequisite for accomplishing this task, the Pentagon needs to develop new doctrine and rules of engagement for protecting civilians from mass atrocities and genocide. Doctrine establishes principles to guide the actions of the military in the pursuit of national objectives. As noted by the Genocide Prevention Task Force, there is no comprehensive doctrine in the American defense establishment for protecting civilians under imminent threat of violence and there are no specific rules of engagement or training that directly address civilian protection. Highlighting these deficiencies, a 2006 Henry L. Stimson Center publication, *The Impossible Mandate: Military Preparedness, the Responsibility to Protect, and Modern Peace Operations*, argues: "If genocide occurs, many forces lack a recognizable strategy to act, since mass violence is not assumed to be a major threat for most peacekeeping operations and its prevention lies outside their usual goals." Traditional peacekeeping strategies no longer apply to the increasingly common need for "coercive protection" activities when combatants make civilians their primary targets. The secretary of defense and the joint chiefs must recognize these changed circumstances and outline a defense doctrine that includes clear guidelines for civilian protection.

It is imperative that military personnel be trained to implement this new civilian protection doctrine. While training exercises and lesson plans have been produced for stabilization operations, such as the 1998 stability and support operations training support package on the use of force, specific training for protecting civilians under threat has never been a central focus of these lesson plans. The 2005 Department of Defense Directive on Military Support for Stability, Security, Transition, and Reconstruction made providing security and humanitarian assistance for civilian populations a core activity of the US forces; this directive should be expanded to include training the military to deal with mass atrocity scenarios.

If military leaders don't see [preventing] genocide, mass atrocities, crimes against humanity as something they may be asked to do, then they're unlikely to do advanced planning for it. They are also unlikely to train in advance for these scenarios, to build guidelines, doctrine, to do simulations, to have their own knowledge on these issues.

Victoria Holt, former senior associate, Future of Peace Operations Program, Henry L. Stimson Center

Traditional peacekeeping and peace building activities have concentrated heavily on finding political solutions to conflict among warring parties. In traditional UN peacekeeping operations, military contingents play observer and monitoring roles for the implementation of political agreements on ceasefires, demobilization, and power-sharing for newly formed governments, but humanitarian initiatives aimed at protecting civilians under threat have not been prioritized. Moving towards a forward-leaning and effective civilian protection doctrine will require a conceptual and operational distinction between protecting civilians and traditional peacekeeping activities in order to distinguish among different operational mandates, particularly those concentrating on humanitarian goals versus those pursuing political objectives. These civilian protection training programs must incorporate doctrine and rules of engagement based on lessons from past cases and contemporary ones, such as Darfur and the DRC.

## CANADA

*The Government of Canada should establish a Canadian Prevention Corps.*
Resources and leadership are needed to operationalize civilian capacity and ensure that Canada contributes to international peace and security. The creation of a multidisciplinary civilian corps focused on preventing mass atrocities would represent a forward-looking shift in Canadian policy.

Canada has a history of leadership on key international initiatives aimed at preventing mass atrocities and indiscriminate loss of civilian lives, including the Ottawa Treaty to Ban Landmines, *The Responsibility to Protect* report, and the Rome Treaty authorizing the creation of the International Criminal Court. While these Canadian-led initiatives are important, it is striking that so little has been done to increase Canada's operational capacity to enable leadership in the prevention of mass atrocities.

We have this huge ship of state now, the Department of
Foreign Affairs and International Trade, that doesn't turn
fast enough whereas tiny countries like Norway, Finland,
and Denmark have little ships adapting or reacting very
quickly to crises. We need to have teams of talent available
to seize a crisis and make it our own, and have the will
and the physical and monetary resources to do it. But you
need top people, and where are those? Those top people
are usually taken by top jobs and cannot be freed.

Raymond Chrétien, former Canadian ambassador to the
United States

Canada can make a significant contribution to global security by improving its permanent, standby capacity for preventive
action. A Canadian Prevention Corps would enable the Government of Canada to deploy a team of dedicated civil servants
from anywhere in the government. The United States has moved
in this direction with the creation of a Civilian Response Corps
to support stabilization missions. The Canadian Prevention
Corps would provide a critical mass of multidisciplinary experts
to work with high-level special envoys for preventive diplomacy
and fact-finding missions. The corps should be civilian-led and
operate under the aegis of the proposed international security
minister; it should be drawn from the ranks of DFAIT, CIDA,
Health Canada, the Royal Canadian Mounted Police, Finance
Canada, Justice Canada, Elections Canada, and the Department
of National Defence. These experts would apply to join the corps
on a full-time basis from their respective departments. The corps
should fall under the responsibility of the proposed Coordinating Office for the Prevention of Mass Atrocities.

*The Government of Canada should increase its diplomatic and development
presence in fragile countries.*
A modernized and robust foreign service is essential to any
Canadian effort to operationalize the responsibility to protect.

Canada needs to increase the recruitment and training of Foreign Service officers and increase its diplomatic and development presence in vulnerable countries. This critical investment would augment Canada's diplomatic capacity to monitor countries for early warning signs such as hate propaganda, suspicious arms shipments, political extremism, exclusivist nationalism, and state discrimination on ethnic, religious, political, or gender grounds.

Of vital importance is the need to redress the budget reductions that have undermined the foreign service for more than two decades. Indeed, throughout the 1980s the Progressive Conservative government reduced the total number of Foreign Affairs staff by almost twenty per cent. Further cuts by the Liberal government in the 1990s slashed the department's budget and total number of staff by twenty-five per cent and thirteen per cent respectively. Andrew Cohen's 2003 book, *While Canada Slept*, noted that Foreign Service officers accounted for only fifteen per cent of DFAIT's staff members. Of the country's 164 diplomatic missions, close to half were staffed by three or fewer Canadians. The severe understaffing of Canada's diplomatic missions – particularly in developing countries – has overburdened Foreign Service officers with administrative work and compromised their ability to conduct detailed political analysis.

According to current plans, by the 2010–11 fiscal year, DFAIT's budget will be reduced by CAN$639 million. In contrast, DND's budget will be increased by more than CAN$1.9 billion. The increase in funding allocations for DND needs to be matched across government departments if Canada's diplomatic capacity is to be rejuvenated. We recommend funding to increase the number of diplomats and to develop comprehensive training programs on the broad skills of negotiation and preventive diplomacy.

As a key component of a national prevention strategy, in contrast to existing practices at DFAIT, regional specialization must be encouraged among diplomats. Diplomats need to be trained in country-specific economic, demographic, social, and environmental trends, in addition to language, culture, history, and politics. Moreover, both senior diplomats and new hires should be trained on the responsibility to protect. Very few diplomatic officials in the Canadian government were experts on Somalia in 1992, Rwanda in 1994, or Afghanistan in 2001. This lack of regional expertise was detrimental to Canada's decision making in all three of these Canadian engagements. While Canada continues to develop considerable knowledge on Afghanistan, country-specific expertise needs to be developed as part of a coordinated strategy. Canadian diplomats should specialize before a crisis erupts rather than afterwards.

The Canadian government should pursue an international development policy that ties assistance to the long-term strategic goal of preventing mass atrocities. CIDA should increase and target development assistance to reach countries where the threat of mass atrocities is most likely. Development, if conducted strategically, can alleviate the structural conditions that engender violence and repression. Economic growth and development, when wisely planned, reduce poverty and inequality by generating employment opportunities for youth in vulnerable countries. This, in turn, reduces the recruitment of unemployed and disaffected youth into radical movements or criminal gangs while decreasing large-scale illegal migration.

> If we believe that all humans are human, then how are we going to prove it? It can only be proven through our actions. Through the dollars we are prepared to expend to improve conditions in the Third World, through the time and energy we devote to solving devastating problems, like AIDS, through the lives of our soldiers, which we are prepared to sacrifice for the sake of humanity.
>
> Roméo Dallaire, Lieutenant-General (Retired) and Canadian senator

Canada's traditional approach to development is undergoing significant change. On 23 February 2009, CIDA announced that its bilateral assistance program will prioritize twenty recipient countries. The new list of countries reflects a stronger focus on enhancing trade links with Latin America, while African countries, including Benin, Burkina Faso, Cameroon, Kenya, Malawi, Niger, Rwanda, Burundi, and Zambia, were removed. This new policy departs from Canada's traditional emphasis on reducing poverty in the world's poorest countries. Moreover, *Foreign Policy* magazine's "Failed States Index" identifies Kenya and Rwanda as countries at risk of new mass atrocities. It is counter-intuitive that CIDA is turning away from Africa at a time when the continent remains acutely vulnerable to the pressures of climate change, rapid demographic growth, poverty, and social inequality – the very conditions that give rise to mass atrocities.

CIDA's shift toward the Americas also weakens a long-standing principle of Canadian development policy in which the government has traditionally strengthened national unity by devoting attention to the French-speaking world through La Francophonie, an international organization linking francophone nations around the world. Canadian development assistance was often allocated equitably between English and French-speaking countries in Africa and the Caribbean.

CIDA should undertake a thorough reassessment of its aid policy and renew its commitment to the world's most vulnerable countries. Steps should be taken to post a larger number of CIDA officials in fragile countries. A Senate committee, chaired by Senator Hugh Segal, released a report in 2007 titled *Overcoming 40 Years of Failure: A New Road Map for Sub-Saharan Africa*, which noted that eighty-one per cent of CIDA's 1,500 employees are based in Ottawa. The report advocated increasing the number of CIDA personnel outside Canada to augment the effectiveness of Canadian aid and to strengthen regional specialization.

At the time [in 1994], we never had an embassy in Burundi, we never had an embassy in Rwanda, and the embassy in Kinshasa had been closed for two years. So our knowledge of the situation on the ground was extremely spotty.

Louis Delvoie, former assistant deputy minister, Department of National Defence

Placing more CIDA officers overseas should be followed by an increase in aid for the troubled corners of the world. Although the Conservative government has pledged to increase Canada's official development assistance by eight per cent per year, as of 2009 the amount pledged remains at 0.32 per cent of gross national product, or CAN$4.8 billion. The government must take steps to meet the target of 0.7 per cent, which the Canadian Parliament endorsed in a June 2005 vote.

*The Government of Canada should continue enhancing the Canadian Forces' capabilities by increasing its force strength and developing operational concepts, doctrine, force structure, and training to support civilian protection.*

Over the past two decades, civilians have become a growing target of violence. The shift towards low-technology, high-casualty, intrastate conflict necessitates a reorientation of the Canadian Forces' approach to peace operations. During operations, the Canadian Forces have been repeatedly exposed to, and required to operate within, an environment that has been termed the "three block war." In this paradigm, a detachment engages in high-intensity combat on one block; on the second block, a detachment interposes itself between two hostile mobs; and on the third block, another detachment from the same unit secures humanitarian space for the delivery of aid and the protection of civilians. While the Canadian Forces have led the way with new and innovative professional development facilities like the Peace Support Training Centre, the Canadian Maneuver Training Centre, and simulation centers across the country, the protection of civilians needs to be institutionalized throughout the military. Canada's military forces must develop operational concepts, establish doctrine, design a force structure, and conduct extensive and effective training for civilian protection.

Canada has reduced its military capabilities over the past few decades. The government's decision to cut the military's budget in the early 1990s was tied to the belief that the end of the Cold War and a sustained period of international peace would yield a significant "peace dividend." These savings reduced the federal deficit but the cuts adversely affected military capability. During this time the Canadian Forces were reduced from 85,000 to approximately 55,000 personnel – a cull which, despite years of budgetary surplus, is only now being remedied. Current and past governments have increased defence spending, developed a whole-of-government approach to operations, and authorized and funded additional military personnel.

At present the Canadian military is overstretched, with many members serving on multiple tours of duty in Afghanistan. This capacity shortfall is especially acute within UN peacekeeping operations. In 1993, Canada contributed more than 3,000 troops to UN peacekeeping missions, but as of early 2010, it has deployed a historic low of sixty-five Canadian soldiers with the United Nations. Overall, the higher-than-expected attrition of mid-career personnel, who possess valuable expertise and experience, has prevented the Canadian Forces from expanding. The forces are treading water.

The Canadian Forces must be better prepared to confront the new security challenges of the twenty-first century. W21 recommends that the Canadian Forces be allocated sufficient resources to recruit and retain more soldiers to strengthen the military overall – and the land forces in particular – so that Canada can make greater contributions to international peace and security. W21 welcomes the Canada First Defence Strategy, introduced by the Conservative government in 2009, and the pledged 2.7 per cent annual increase in spending to enhance investments in personnel, equipment, readiness, and infrastructure.

A shortage of heavy-lift capacity remains a problem for most middle powers. Few can afford the expensive air equipment needed to project power abroad. Canada is currently building its heavy lift capacity. The government has purchased four Boeing C–17 Globemasters to support its operations in Afghanistan. The aircraft can carry a 43,000-kilogram load, or roughly four-to-five times the capacity of the C–130 aircraft that the Canadian government deployed to serve Rwanda in 1994. The acquisition of the Globemasters has afforded Canada a degree of independence. The military no longer has to borrow US C–17s or rent Soviet-era aircraft to transport Canadian Forces personnel and equipment. Although the C–17 Globemasters are serving

Canada's soldiers in Afghanistan, they have also delivered aid to countries affected by natural disasters.

In addition, the government's proposed acquisition of joint support ships, a new fleet of Hercules transport aircraft (considered "the workhorse" of any future mission), a fleet of heavy lift Chinook helicopters, and new wheeled transport vehicles, will provide the Government of Canada with the capacity to rapidly deploy forces to a mission area by sea, air, or ground. By addressing the size of the military, its rapid deployment capacity, and operational effectiveness in complex and dangerous environments, Canada will ensure it can assume a greater leadership role in civilian protection operations.

> I think our biggest difficulty in overseas operations is capability. And if we had more capability, available capability at our fingertips, we would be more likely to intervene... You have to have the ability to get where you want to go, and put enough people on the ground and support them, which in some cases is a lot more difficult than it looks.
>
> Ken Calder, former assistant deputy minister, Department of National Defence

### ENSURING KNOWLEDGE

The failure of civil society and the news media to exert sustained pressure on the American and Canadian governments has been a central obstacle to preventing mass atrocities. As the Rwandan Genocide demonstrated, politicians often cannot be relied upon to act of their own volition. Rather, a vocal and broad-based constituency must emerge with the ability to advocate the case for governmental action in a persuasive manner.

To achieve preventive action, non-state actors must improve their exchange of information and develop enhanced strategies to engage politicians at the executive and legislative levels. Civil society groups and the national news media have enormous potential to influence decision makers, and play a critical role in spreading public awareness of mass atrocities and their consequences for international security. Individual activists and civil society organizations can generate interest inside and outside government by writing editorials, participating in television, radio and print interviews, sponsoring letter writing and educational campaigns, and staging public protests.

The term "civil society" denotes individuals, organizations, and community groups that are non-state and non-commercial. The diversity of civil society organizations brings to public policy a highly varied body of expertise, knowledge, and field experience from around the world. Large NGOs such as Oxfam, CARE, Save the Children, Human Rights Watch, and Amnesty International, which maintain offices in the United States, Canada, and around the globe, are often the most visible civil society groups acting on humanitarian and human rights issues. Some of these NGOs, notably Human Rights Watch and Oxfam, have promoted the responsibility to protect since it was articulated in 2001 and remain committed to making this concept a key doctrine of American and Canadian foreign policy.

> You have a change in context between now and Rwanda in the sense that there are just more NGOs around the world and foundations around the world with more endowments than we've ever had before, so government is more than ever before one of many stakeholders.
>
> Jared Cohen, author of *One Hundred Days of Silence: America and the Rwanda Genocide*

In addition to these high-profile NGOs, grassroots activism by charitable foundations, faith-based, diaspora, student, senior citizen, and veteran groups are vital to mobilizing the will to intervene for the prevention of mass atrocities. These groups can engage specific constituencies and mobilize support in communities across our two nations for the prevention of mass atrocities. National organizations need to increase their cooperation with grassroots groups to mount broad-based campaigns on this vital issue.

The "fourth estate" – the news media – exerts a powerful influence on government. The "CNN effect" is credited with persuading the US and Canadian governments to intervene in Somalia in 1992, Bosnia in 1995, and eastern Zaire in 1996. Policy experts argue that the process of "policy by media," or formulating policy in response to media coverage, is a contemporary phenomenon that arises from the government's sensitivity to media coverage. While news media reports influence policy, the inverse is also true: an absence of reporting on mass atrocities in a particular country removes the pressure on the American and Canadian governments to act on their responsibility to protect. The paucity of media coverage devoted to the Rwandan Genocide in April 1994 enabled American and Canadian officials to cite a lack of public pressure as a justification for their weak-willed responses.

Civil society groups and the news media must acknowledge the importance of their power and responsibility to mobilize local and national constituencies at election time to protect groups threatened by mass atrocities and to help the public understand the connections between their own self-interest and the interests of people living in vulnerable societies overseas. To this end, the following section combines strategic and practical recommendations for American and Canadian civil society groups, as well as news media organizations, to improve their effectiveness in influencing government policy.

### Civil Society

*American and Canadian civil society organizations should develop permanent domestic constituencies by forming national coalitions for the responsibility to protect in the United States and Canada.*

Broad-based national coalitions are vital to forging the political will needed to prevent mass atrocities. Perhaps more than any issue, preventing genocide and other mass atrocities has the potential to overcome divides between NGOs, faith-based, and diaspora groups, while helping them to build bridges with think-tanks and academic institutions.

The International Coalition for the Responsibility to Protect is working to establish a permanent international network of NGOs to promote the principles of R2P at the United Nations and regional and sub-regional governmental bodies around the world. The International Coalition and one of its partners, the Global Centre for the Responsibility to Protect, both of which are based in New York, are mandated to work around the world to move R2P "from principle to practice." At present, however, no coalitions exist in the United States or Canada to mobilize domestic support and build a broad network of American and Canadian NGOs to lobby our governments for the implementation of the responsibility to protect.

When I worked in the White House, every time we wanted to do something on an issue like Congo or Rwanda, we'd turn around and hope that citizens across the country were going to push our issue forward, but there was nothing but a big, big silence. So what we need, all over this country, is people who are willing to stand up and make noise whenever there is a situation that demands the United States' attention and our action.

John Prendergast, co-chair, the Enough Project

Civil society groups in Canada are leading international voices on human rights issues but the gap between Canadian rhetoric and action remains significant. A majority of the representatives of civil society groups and academics who attended a meeting convened by the World Federalist movement in Ottawa in March 2008 agreed on the need to create a domestic network in Canada to normalize the principles of the responsibility to protect. We agree that Canada's civil society groups should form a domestic network of organizations and activists to buttress the efforts of the International Coalition on R2P. The proposed Canadian coalition for R2P should organize a national advocacy campaign that engages grassroots organizations and attracts national support, raises awareness among the public and in Parliament, attracts national and local media attention, lobbies the government for prevention policy, and, as necessary, advocates specific actions to prevent or interdict mass atrocities on a case-by-case basis. The coalition's headquarters should be based in Ottawa to facilitate lobbying of the federal government, while advocating for the responsibility to protect throughout the country.

In their anti-genocide campaigns, civil society groups in America have been more active and successful than their Canadian counterparts. NGOs such as Save Darfur and the Genocide Intervention Network, and think-tanks such as the Center for American Progress, the Brookings Institution, the Henry L. Stimson Center and the United States Institute for Peace, are promoting stronger civilian protection policies. These groups have started to build the critical mass of support necessary to influence US policy. The W2I Project proposes the creation of a US coalition for the responsibility to protect, based in Washington DC, charged with coordinating civil society groups in a united campaign for the prevention of mass atrocities. With a permanent lobby in Washington, the coalition would pressure the executive and legislative branches to develop effective prevention and response policies. The so-called "prevention pillar" – the most important aspect of the responsibility to protect – would provide a platform for consensus among members of the coalition, leading to a formidable lobbying partnership. The national coalition would also educate the public about the responsibility to protect and monitor ongoing conflicts and regions at risk.

Increasingly, as our own population becomes more diverse …the old Methodist values handed down by Lester Pearson no longer apply. We had the Trudeau Jesuits and now we've got the diasporas, which are much more conservative,

> clearly much more engaged in issues affecting their home-
> lands. They increasingly play a role, and probably will
> more and more, as they become more [powerful], not just
> in demographics, but more politically smart, better off.
> They're sophisticated in their roles, and much stronger
> lobbyists now.
>
> Lloyd Axworthy, former Canadian minister of foreign affairs

The Canadian coalition for the responsibility to protect would
be wise to incorporate faith-based organizations, with their long
history of activism, into the movement for genocide prevention.
Project Ploughshares, a Canadian church-based organization
that works on peace and security issues, has stood at the forefront of R2P activism in Canada. However, faith-based groups in
Canada have not enjoyed as much success as their sister groups
in the United States. Canadian religious groups should draw
lessons from the work of American faith-based groups, which
have raised domestic awareness of the plight of civilians in Darfur. In July 2008, Save Darfur attracted considerable support
from faith-based groups and decision makers from across the
United States by organizing a weekend of reflection and prayer
for the people of Darfur. For their part, the Friends Committee on National Legislation, the lobbying arm of the Quakers in
the United States, has released a policy document entitled *The
Responsibility to Prevent*, which encourages Congress to institutionalize the prevention of mass atrocities.

Coalitions uniting the young and old in the campaign for
the prevention of mass atrocities would be especially valuable.
Cooperation between Canadian student groups, such as STAND
– the student-led division of the Genocide Intervention Network
– or Save Darfur, could work side by side with senior citizens'
groups such as the Raging Grannies, an organization of retired
women dedicated to promoting social justice. The potential synergies and impacts are great. Politicians pay attention when so
many votes are at stake.

In the United States, the Genocide Intervention Network has been a source of innovative activism, developing "scorecards" that grade members of Congress on their voting records and their leadership regarding Darfur. The network has also created a hotline that connects callers to the offices of their members of Congress free of charge, providing a convenient channel for voters to communicate their concerns. A similar strategy would be effective in Canada and should be adopted by Canadian civil society organizations.

The creation of the US and Canadian coalitions with offices in Washington and Ottawa will help to establish permanent constituencies for the responsibility to protect across North America. Lobbyists for R2P in our national capitals will amplify the voices of grassroots community activists by organizing constituent visits with legislators in the capitals and their home districts. National coalition staff would have the funds to commission focus group studies and targeted attitude survey research on the responsibility to protect. The ability to deploy these and many other techniques commonly used by lobbyists will put to work new synergies for preventing genocide and mass atrocity crimes.

*American and Canadian civil society organizations should expand their advocacy by targeting local/municipal and state/provincial levels of government to support the principles of the responsibility to protect.*

In recent years, civil society groups have increasingly undertaken creative initiatives targeting politicians at the state and provincial levels to influence foreign policy. For example, the R2P Coalition, an American NGO, borrowing from the environmental movement, has successfully campaigned for the adoption of resolutions supporting the principles of the responsibility to protect at the municipal and state levels of government. Pressure by the R2P Coalition moved the Illinois General Assembly, the city of Chicago, and the city of San Francisco to pass resolutions supporting the responsibility to protect. The success of the R2P Coalition demonstrates particularly the value of targeting municipal-level decision makers in urban centers. If well covered by local and national media, municipal and state level campaigns bring national attention to R2P principles. Large American cities like New York, Boston, Washington, Los Angeles, Miami, and Atlanta are gateways to the world, enlightened and outward looking, but increasingly vulnerable to threats arising from conflict zones that have fallen off the world's radar screens. Shared space means shared destiny. Whether it is passengers carrying infectious diseases flying into international airports, criminal activities, terrorism, or economic disruptions, local actions have global consequences and it is in our enlightened self-interest to prevent mass atrocities. W21's message that our governments must develop national strategies for the prevention of genocide and mass atrocity crimes will resonate particularly with the residents of these major cities.

Canada's predominantly international approach to advocacy for the responsibility to protect has meant that its NGOs often concentrate on making headway at the United Nations and at the international level. However, Canadian NGOs should not overlook the political importance of municipal councils and provincial legislatures. Civil society groups in Canada should emulate the strategy pursued by their American counterparts, with special emphasis on lobbying municipal governments in large urban centers such as Toronto, Montreal, Vancouver, Ottawa, and Calgary. Nor should we neglect lobbying the legislatures of the four largest provinces in Canada – Ontario, Quebec, British Columbia, and Alberta – home to eighty-six per cent of Canada's population.

According to the famous advice that the late Congressman Tip O'Neill received from his father, "all politics is local." NGOs, civil society, and communities must work in their own backyards. Once municipal councils and state/provincial legislatures speak strongly in favor of making the responsibility to protect a new norm, federal politicians will listen.

*American and Canadian civil society groups should develop strategic, outcome-based proposals geared towards key decision makers in government.*

Civil society groups must present a practical and persuasive message to the decision makers they seek to influence. Groups must move beyond well-meaning but simplistic calls for the government to "do something" to prevent mass atrocities and provide precise proposals for action founded on results-based analysis. Civil society groups should assemble experts and activists to develop strategic policy proposals framed as practical solutions for politicians and civil servants. A results-based approach can move advocacy beyond drawing attention to an issue to providing political leaders with policy proposals that are attuned to the country's capabilities. Strategic proposals should contain specific assessments of crises and suggest appropriate responses. Proposals should analyze the resources and capabilities at the disposal of the US or Canadian government, outline the long-term and short-term political, security, and financial consequences of action versus inaction, and tailor proposed action strategies accordingly. The old approaches of either putting the burden of coming up with a solution exclusively on the government, or calling on the government for actions that are ill-conceived or unrealistic and then walking away from the problem, are as ineffective as they are irresponsible.

Advocates must target all levels of government. The executive level is often the most difficult to reach but is the most influential. The executive is critical to generating urgent government responses to breaking crises, while the civil service is vital to affecting long-term prevention policies. It is imperative that advocates build and sustain long-term relationships with key civil servants, politicians, and members of the executive, so that they may strategically reach all levels of government with their proposals for action. Above all, it is essential that advocates have a firm understanding of the machinery of government and the roles of the relevant decision makers before they propose policy changes to government.

Garnering political support within the US Congress and the Parliament of Canada is vital for advocates. Appeals to the legislative branch should emphasize widespread public support for preventing mass atrocities. Local town hall meetings with legislators, phone and letter writing campaigns, petitions, and opinion polls can demonstrate high levels of public support for prevention policies and responsive actions. Advocates may communicate to legislators that they will lose electoral support if they are on the wrong side of the issue. Sympathetic legislators should propose hearings on proposals for preventive strategies and actions. In Congress, the Tom Lantos Human Rights Commission and the proposed Caucus on the Prevention of Mass Atrocities would be appropriate forums for presenting strategic proposals. In Parliament, W21's proposed standing joint committee for the prevention of genocide, the House of Commons Standing Committee on Foreign Affairs and International Development, and the Senate Standing Committee on National Security and Defence provide venues for expert testimony and the presentation of strategic proposals.

*American and Canadian civil society groups should leverage new information and communications technologies to educate the public and government.*

Since the 1994 Rwandan Genocide, the world has undergone a communications revolution. The meteoric rise of communications technologies has enabled a wide range of actors and organizations to communicate critical information efficiently, cheaply, and immediately. NGO field workers are in an extraordinary position to use this technology to provide eyewitness information to governments, the news media, and the public.

Governments and media outlets around the world frequently ask Human Rights Watch to provide them with on-the-ground reports from some of the world's most conflict-ridden locations. The web sites of Human Rights Watch and the International Crisis Group provide useful links to analytical reports, videos, and photographs gathered from areas that the mainstream North American news media underreport. Human Rights Watch's ability to collect and disseminate news on human rights violations has been a boon to civil society groups focused on human rights issues and needs to be duplicated more widely by civil society groups dedicated to the prevention of mass atrocities.

> If the Internet had existed [during Rwanda], what would
> have been the case? What would have happened if we had
> been in the state of information technology that we are
> now? I don't know, but I think we are in a different world.
> At that point, the media didn't do as much as it should've.
> If it were to perform at the same level today, it might not
> be so serious because there are so many other ways to get
> information out.
>
> Alison Des Forges, former senior advisor to the Africa divi-
> sion at Human Rights Watch

Cell phones can upload digital images to the Internet in seconds
– just one of the developments that now facilitates communication among NGOs, the news media, and the public. Inexpensive
camcorders such as flip cams can capture an hour or more of
broadcast-quality digital video. Media outlets seeking eyewitness
reports are using video and audio gathered by NGOs more than
ever before. Seizing the opportunity, NGOs have encouraged the
growth of "video advocacy." Organizations such as WITNESS, an
NGO founded by musician Peter Gabriel and based in New York,
now train aid workers and activists to capture visual evidence of
human rights violations around the world and upload the footage to the web to generate public awareness. These innovations
have equipped civil society groups with the ability to communicate directly with the public and attract the attention of the
image-centric news media at a relatively low cost. Even if news
agencies choose not to use documentation provided by NGOs, the
powerful images they convey sometimes prompt the dispatch of
reporters to cover the story.

> We're very aware of the fact that the major networks have
> cut back substantially in their international coverage. If
> you are going to be on TV these days, you have to supply

the video. If there's not a video provided there's not a story. In places like Darfur, early on we physically had to provide the video or we had to drag a TV crew in. The first time we were on ABC it was because we provided the video. The first time we got on CNN, it is because we dragged them in, driving across the border from Chad.

Kenneth Roth, executive director, Human Rights Watch

As communications technologies become increasingly sophisticated and affordable, online crisis reporting presents another opportunity for civil society to mobilize political will. For example, Ushahidi is an innovative web site that "crowd-sources crisis information" by publishing citizen "reports" from crisis hotspots, which can be submitted via e-mail or text message. The web site aggregates the reports as geographic points in Google maps. New user-friendly communications innovations such as YouTube, Yahoo's "You Witness News," Facebook, and Twitter can serve as effective online channels for civil society groups to engage in reporting, advocacy, and networking.

*American and Canadian civil society groups should initiate public discussions on the prevention of mass atrocities and related foreign policy issues.*
The United States and Canada have a multitude of non-partisan think-tanks and research centers that produce well-researched policy recommendations aimed at governments. These groups can claim successes in raising public and government awareness about mass atrocities, including the attention brought to Darfur. However, NGOs and other civil society groups should expand their efforts to organize public discussions about preventing mass atrocities, so as to build and enlarge genocide prevention constituencies and provide a forum for citizens' questions and concerns.

The Aurea Foundation is a Toronto-based charitable foundation founded by Peter and Melanie Munk that hosts national policy debates in Canada on subjects such as humanitarian intervention and global security. The public can watch the debates live at selected movie theatres across Canada or download the videos or transcripts from the foundation's web site. These debates have featured high-profile speakers including Richard Holbrooke, Mia Farrow, John Bolton, Charles Krauthammer, Samantha Power, Rick Hillier, and Gareth Evans. The Canadian Broadcasting Corporation and *The Globe and Mail* newspaper cover the debates, encouraging public participation and disseminating the ideas under discussion. Civil society groups should view these debates as a model for public awareness campaigns.

In addition, universities are increasingly playing a role in staging discussions on foreign policy and making them available to the wider public. The Morris J. Wosk Centre for Dialogue at Simon Fraser University in Vancouver has initiated a three-year project entitled "Canada's World," with the aim of engaging citizens on Canadian foreign policy. This initiative's primary activities include roundtable discussions, interviews, regional dialogues, online exchanges, and a concluding national discussion. Participants include academics, business leaders, NGOs, public servants, youth organizations, and diaspora groups. This initiative illustrates how civil society can be brought together to engage on foreign policy issues.

In another example of creative engagement by civil society organizations, the Center for American Progress' Enough Project funded a tour of Darfur and northern Uganda, hosted by Enough Project co-chair Jon Prendergast and *Hotel Rwanda* star Don Cheadle. The tour constituted a novel approach to sparking public interest and discussion on Darfur and achieved an outpouring of interest throughout the United States.

Up-to-date communications technologies are enhancing the ability of civil society groups in the United States and Canada to foster national public debate at a relatively low cost. NGOs based in Quebec, such as Oxfam Québec, should be at the forefront of these initiatives to expand and tailor the discussions to francophone audiences. The remarkable shift from the American public's limited engagement during the Rwandan Genocide to today's widespread support for action on Darfur can be largely attributed to the success of public awareness campaigns spearheaded by NGOs. By fostering more civil society-led debates on genocide prevention and linking it to the national interest of Canada and the United States, civil society groups can raise public awareness and mobilize the will to intervene at the highest levels of government.

## News Media

*Individual journalists, media owners, and managers in the United States and Canada should commit themselves to "the responsibility to report."*
In liberal democracies, the news media play the crucial role of keeping the public informed and holding the government accountable for its actions. The media relay images and information from across the globe to inform audiences of political developments and humanitarian crises. Domestically they act as the public's eyes and ears in the halls of power. At their best, the news media report current events and provide in-depth analysis so that the public can make informed choices.

The contemporary news media – including print, television and radio broadcasting, and online journalism – are in a period of rapid transition. The recent global economic crisis, coupled with competition from online advertising, have shaken the traditional news business model to its core. Local television news stations and newspapers across the United States and Canada are laying off staff and struggling to remain profitable, and major newspapers such as the *Seattle Post-Intelligencer* have been forced to publish exclusively online. These changes to the journalism industry are unlikely to diminish the significance of professional journalists, who will continue to influence American and Canadian foreign policy through emerging online and non-profit news models.

Individual journalists are extraordinarily important in mobilizing governmental action. The CNN effect suggests that the news media's influence on public opinion, through reports and images, is powerful enough to force the government to re-evaluate its policy priorities. This phenomenon was evident in the US decision to launch Operation Provide Comfort in 1991 – a humanitarian relief operation undertaken in response to widespread media coverage of the suffering of Kurdish refugees in northern

Iraq. The CNN effect has also had demonstrably negative effects on the government's perception of public attitudes. For example, in October 1993 televised images of clan fighters dragging a US Ranger's body through the streets of Mogadishu caused President Clinton to announce the withdrawal of US troops from Somalia – a decision now widely viewed as ill-considered.

> If a genocide is going on, does the media have a responsibility to cover it? Does the media have any responsibility to participate in the notion of protection, or is their responsibility to be one more step removed and just cover accurately whether or not anyone is doing it? It's a fascinating question because you'll get a lot of journalists who will say there are ethics involved in crossing that line. There are ethics, but there are also a lot of dead bodies.
>
> Gayle Smith, former senior fellow, Center for American Progress

Tragically, human rights violations on a mass scale are often not deemed newsworthy by the dominant news agencies. During the perpetration of some of the most egregious mass atrocities in Darfur in 2004 and 2005, US television news networks manifestly failed to fulfill their "responsibility to report." In 2004, the ABC network committed a mere eighteen minutes of airtime to the Darfur conflict, while NBC contributed only five minutes and CBS only three minutes, according to a 2004 Tyndall Report. The same three networks in that same year devoted a total of 130 minutes of airtime to Martha Stewart's trial. According to research by the American Progress Action Fund, in June 2005, the Michael Jackson trial, coverage of a new Tom Cruise film and his relationship with Katie Holmes, and a human interest story about a "runaway bride" garnered more news coverage than all reporting on the crisis in Darfur by ABC, CBS, NBC, CNN, Fox News, and MSNBC combined.

The overall lack of media interest in cases like Darfur should not detract from the exceptional coverage of mass atrocities pursued by individual journalists abroad. As CNN's chief international correspondent, Christiane Amanpour consistently integrated a human rights "angle" into her reports. In Canada, *The Globe and Mail*'s former Africa correspondent, Stephanie Nolen, raised awareness of the devastating impact of HIV/AIDS and armed conflict on the continent. Nicholas Kristof of *The New York Times* has focused on human rights abuses in Asia and Africa and is credited with bringing significant public attention to mass atrocity crimes in Darfur. In 2006, Kristof launched an annual essay contest for American university students in which the winner travels with him to Africa and writes a blog for *The New York Times*. Sadly, however, these are exceptions to the rule.

Journalists can and should exercise individual leadership within their newsrooms to bring attention to mass human rights violations and conditions that lead to mass atrocities. American and Canadian media organizations operate very democratically. It is imperative that senior editors continue to allow reporters considerable freedom and creativity to pursue stories that affect the daily news agenda, and individual journalists must take advantage of this freedom to underscore mass atrocities and politicians' responses at home and abroad.

American and Canadian journalists should pursue innovative opportunities to increase their field-reporting experience in volatile countries and shape a long-term understanding of the world beyond their nation's borders. There are a number of programs designed to help journalists gain this vital international experience. Since 1998, the International Reporting Project at Johns Hopkins University has sent more than 270 journalists to work in over eighty-five countries. Similarly, the Knight International Journalism Fellowships enable journalists from the United States to lead projects in partnership with local media and journalism organizations in countries around the world, where they work to improve media institutions and report on poverty, development, and health issues. The Canadian International Development Agency's Journalism and Development Initiative is another important resource for journalists and organizations to fund foreign reporting projects. Columnists, broadcasters, reporters, and editors should avail themselves of these funding opportunities to train or work abroad, particularly in poor or politically volatile countries.

Within a period of about seven months I had six national press conferences here with members from across party lines dealing with gross human rights abuses. I even pushed for and got opposition party agreement to work together to form a working group sub-committee to deal with crises such as the Congo [DRC] and Sudan. That was accomplished, a press conference was held, a document released. It was a huge amount of effort, and no attention was paid to it. In the six national press conferences that I had, in the sum total of those, one [media] intern was sent, once.

Keith Martin, Canadian member of Parliament

As news agencies face shrinking budgets and dwindling foreign bureaus, there is a growing need for these international perspectives in newsrooms. Today, it is common for reporters to cover outbreaks of deadly violence from their desks in Ottawa, Toronto, Washington, or New York. Reporters may be rapidly "parachuted" into regions to cover major international crises, but this hasty approach leads to coverage deficient in continuity and context. Travel and international experience provides journalists with invaluable insight into the conditions giving rise to conflict and mass atrocities around the world and bolsters the profession's dedication to these issues. Senior editors should recognize the importance of foreign experience to professional development and grant journalists the opportunities for foreign travel. Professional associations such as the Canadian Association of Journalists and the American Newspaper Guild should support programs that encourage professional experience in the world's poorest countries, volatile states, and conflict zones.

Journalism students, who constitute the next generation of reporters, also need the means to travel and gain international experience. University administrators and professors of journalism can play an important leadership role by supporting international training programs. The Berkeley Graduate School of Journalism at the University of California offers an international reporting program dedicated to sending students abroad. In Canada, Carleton University's Rwanda Initiative provides students with valuable experience reporting inside that country. Allan Thompson, a former journalist with the *Toronto Star* and now a professor at Carleton University – who coined the phrase "responsibility to report" – has proposed the creation of a Centre for Media and Transitional Societies to expand the university's foreign training programs for journalism students. At the University of British Columbia, a private philanthropist is funding a new program for students and faculty members to practice journalism overseas, covering underreported stories pertaining to development. Such initiatives are vital to the creation of a new generation of journalists who possess the insight and training necessary to recognize, contextualize, and report signs of mass atrocities.

Professional development programs are an important way to build information-sharing networks among journalists across the globe. Faced with dwindling funding for foreign correspondents, news agencies increasingly rely on "local hires" and freelancers to conduct field research and interviews. Journalists who travel abroad and establish journalism networks in fragile states can maintain collaborative relationships with foreign journalists once they return to Canada and the United States, exchanging raw video and audio, ideas, and information via the Internet. To expand coverage, Canadian and American news agencies can provide links to blogs written by journalists in unstable or war-torn countries and receive up-to-date information relating to risks of mass atrocities. Together, journalists can take a "bottom-up" approach to influencing the content produced by their news organizations, earning critical support for foreign coverage from senior managers. Recognizing their growing cosmopolitan audiences, as well as the responsibility to report, media owners and managers must allocate sufficient resources to bring the world beyond their borders into Canadian and American homes.

Today's uneven and often sporadic coverage of human rights abuses must be replaced by sustained coverage, complemented by a real understanding of how complex international issues relate to American and Canadian interests at home and abroad. Journalists who increase their awareness of the world that they live in will produce more balanced, insightful coverage. It is not good enough for journalists to cover crises by reporting only the failures associated with humanitarian interventions – they must also cover success stories. In the early 1990s, for example, the first phase of the humanitarian intervention in Somalia broke the back of the famine and saved hundreds of thousands of lives. This success story was drowned out by coverage of the eruption of conflict between international peacekeepers and clan fighters seeking to control food aid deliveries.

Journalists who expand their view of the world will take a greater interest in overseas human rights work and legislative or committee initiatives of members of Parliament and members of Congress. It is necessary that journalists report on risks of mass atrocity crimes before a major crisis erupts; they have a crucial role to play in alerting the public and highlighting options for preventive action. Journalists should view themselves as leaders rather than followers and exercise the responsibility to report on the most egregious human rights violations, not just when the house is burning but when the arsonists are preparing to light the match.

## THE WAY FORWARD

The case for the prevention of mass atrocities once rested largely on moral imperatives and upholding international treaties and conventions. Despite the UN Convention for the Prevention and Punishment of the Crime of Genocide and the Geneva Conventions and their subsequent protocols, treaties to which the United States and Canada are signatories, arguments based on morality and legal obligations have not carried sufficient weight to overwhelm the cold statecraft calculations that traditionally inform government notions of the "national interest." One of the most frequently voiced arguments for explaining the international community's failure to halt the Rwandan Genocide derived from government assessments that deeper involvement was not in the national interest and risking the lives of soldiers would diminish electoral support.

So it is perhaps not surprising that, more than fifteen years after the appalling slaughter in Rwanda, the American and Canadian governments still have not developed national strategies for the prevention of mass atrocity crimes. Policy makers continue to cling to an outdated, narrow and traditional view of the national interest that relegates the prevention of atrocities to a second or third tier foreign policy priority.

A modern understanding of the national interest requires a greater emphasis on the prevention of mass atrocities by leaders. In today's unstable and interdependent global environment, the traditional national interest approach to foreign policy is no longer effective. The combined impact of poverty and inequality, rapid demographic growth, nationalism, and climate change drives deadly violence and threatens international peace and security. These underlying structural factors increase the risks of mass atrocities, and the chaos resulting from those atrocities poses credible dangers to American and Canadian national interests at home and abroad. If we continue to deal with looming genocides and other mass atrocities in a reactive manner, we will confront more than just the moral failure to save lives. Inevitably, the United States and Canada will face threats to their own national security and prosperity.

Mass atrocities threaten our domestic security in several ways, including the spread of pandemics. The chaos they create necessitates their prevention as a strategic foreign policy goal serving the national interest. An unfortunate consequence of the recent focus on countries in the Middle East and Central Asia has been a corresponding failure to consider the international effects of conflicts in Africa. Sustained and well-planned strategies are needed to end the worst conflicts on that continent, particularly in the DRC. The ongoing conflict in eastern DRC has already led to public health crises that have the potential to escalate into epidemics and pandemics. The United States and Canada cannot afford to tolerate the human suffering that massively destabilizes African countries simply because they lie beyond our traditional and short-term understanding of the national interest.

The lessons learned from the international community's failure to halt the Rwandan Genocide in 1994 and the humanitarian disasters it triggered in the DRC led to the NATO military intervention in Kosovo in 1999. These two defining cases inaugurated humanitarian intervention as a necessary guarantor of international security and opened a policy window that enabled the formulation of the responsibility to protect. Unfortunately, budding support for legitimate humanitarian intervention has been undermined since the events of 9/11. Military commitments in Iraq and Afghanistan and a coincident global recession have preoccupied decision makers in Washington and Ottawa, further relegating the prevention of mass atrocities to the margins. But competing priorities are no excuse for inaction. In fact, they underscore the vital importance of implementing strategies to force the issue of the prevention of mass atrocities onto the radar screens of our governments. This book aims to persuade leaders in Washington and Ottawa that timely and well-informed preventive action can decrease the likelihood and severity of future genocides and mass atrocities.

Our research and interviews identify new approaches for mobilizing political will in support of genocide prevention policies in the United States and Canada. This book asserts that the lack of political will is mutable. Mobilizing political will is a continual process that must be cultivated within and outside of government. The four elements identified as essential to creating the political will to prevent genocide and mass atrocities are leadership from the executive and legislative branches of government, interdepartmental coordination within the government, well-developed civilian and military capacity, and knowledge-sharing and pressure by civil society groups and the news media to raise awareness among decision makers and the public. These foundations need to be strengthened in tandem for the principles of the responsibility to protect to be implemented.

There are two central approaches to generating domestic political will to prevent and interdict mass atrocities. The first is political leadership from the highest levels of government, as exemplified by the US and Canadian governments in Kosovo in 1999. The second is to take a "bottom-up" approach, whereby grassroots groups, NGOs, and activists build a movement for a cause, attracting support from legislators and the media. For this approach to succeed, interest groups must create a permanent constituency and engage the political process. As *The Responsibility to Protect* report states: "Leaders are the ultimate decision makers and they react based on political interests." Civil society groups focused on preventing mass atrocities can reshape the calculation of the national interest and the self-interest of politicians by directing their advocacy towards the government, the news media, and elected officials.

If the responsibility to protect is to become a practical reality, civil society groups in the United States and Canada must coalesce to form a united "will to intervene" movement. This movement should work tirelessly to educate decision makers and the public to persuade them that mass atrocities are both a national security and a humanitarian threat. Civil society groups should lobby for the W21 recommendations among politicians, civil servants, and the public; they should push for the creation of new bodies in the legislative and executive branches of government, where their voices and expertise can inform key decision makers. These vital steps will transform the short-term political calculations that today characterize responses to mass atrocities and begin a long-term policy shift in favor of preventive action. Our national security depends on it.

Driven by the ethical and pragmatic considerations of a middle power, Canadian diplomats have made major contributions to regional and international organizations, including La Francophonie, the G8, the Commonwealth, NATO, and the United Nations; Canadians have won a fine reputation as mediators and reliable allies. Canada has also been at the forefront of the responsibility to protect movement, but there remains a significant gap between its rhetoric and the actions it has taken to embed the

R2P principles within government policy making. As a non-colonial power with a heterogeneous population, Canada should harness its linguistic, ethnic, and religious diversity to promote the prevention of mass atrocities and build a unified front with its allies against the most egregious crimes known to humanity.

The United States is without doubt the most powerful country on the globe; it possesses an unprecedented ability to enable peace and make war. While firmly retaining its commitment to individual freedom and democracy at home, the pendulum of US foreign policy has swung from isolationism to assertive multilateralism to unilateralism and back on more than one occasion. In a globalized world, isolationism is no longer possible and unilateralism is no longer effective. Recognition of the growing interdependence of national economies, security, and public health underscores the necessity of acting collectively. As the unofficial leader of every major international organization in the world, the priorities of the United States enable or constrain the actions of other states. Although the United States has the ability to prevent mass atrocities and intervene in cases of genocide, in contemporary history it has at best assumed an ad hoc reactive stance and at worst remained a bystander to mass murder. Now is the time for the United States to reverse this failure and signal that mass atrocity crimes will not be tolerated by the world's greatest superpower.

By including the prevention of mass atrocities within the national interest, we will move closer to the goal of enshrining prevention as a key foreign policy pillar. The key to mobilizing international support to prevent mass atrocities is to first garner domestic support. This was one of the central arguments of *The Responsibility to Protect*. Mobilizing the will to intervene in North America is the crucial first step towards building international political will and engaging other countries to collectively prevent future mass atrocities.

# APPENDICES

# Summary of W2I Policy Recommendations

A focused set of policy recommendations tailored to improve the US and Canadian governments' planning to prevent mass atrocities are listed below under three rubrics: enabling leadership, enhancing coordination, and building capacity. Under a fourth rubric, ensuring knowledge, we set forth recommendations directed towards civil society organizations and the news media with a view to strengthening their ability to influence government policy. Pressure from civil society organizations and the news media is essential when governments do not exercise the "responsibility to protect" on their own.

## SUMMARY POLICY RECOMMENDATIONS FOR THE GOVERNMENT OF THE UNITED STATES

*Enabling Leadership*
• The president of the United States should issue an executive order establishing the prevention of mass atrocities as a policy priority.
• The US Congress should create a Caucus for the Prevention of Mass Atrocities.
• Members of the US Congress should take individual initiative and use their existing powers and privileges to advocate for the implementation of the responsibility to protect.
• The US Government should foster public discussions on preventing mass atrocities.

*Enhancing Coordination*
• The president should create an Atrocities Prevention Committee to coordinate interagency policy on the prevention of mass
atrocities.
• The national security advisor should create an Interagency
Policy Committee on Preventing Mass Atrocities to coordinate
policy across the executive branch and liaise with the Atrocities
Prevention Committee.
• The national security advisor should create standard operating
procedures for disseminating intelligence on the risks of genocide and other mass atrocities.

*Building Capacity*
• The US Government should allocate federal funding to institutionalize the prevention of mass atrocities within civilian
agencies.
• The US Government should re-establish its soft power capacity by expanding its diplomatic and development corps and
enhancing the field training of USAID and State Department
officials.
• The Department of Defense should develop and incorporate doctrine and rules of engagement for preventing and
responding to mass atrocities and train the US military in civilian protection.

---

### SUMMARY POLICY RECOMMENDATIONS FOR THE
### GOVERNMENT OF CANADA

*Enabling Leadership*
• The prime minister should make preventing mass atrocities a
national priority for Canada.
• The prime minister should appoint an international security
minister as a senior member of the Cabinet.
• The Government of Canada should support and promote pub-
lic discussion on Canada's role in preventing mass atrocities.
• The Parliament of Canada should convert the All-Party Par-
liamentary Group for the Prevention of Genocide and Other
Crimes Against Humanity into a standing joint committee.

• Parliamentarians should exercise individual initiative and use their existing powers and privileges to advocate the implementation of the responsibility to protect as an international norm and a vital part of Canada's foreign policy.

*Enhancing Coordination*
• The Government of Canada should create an interdepartmental Coordinating Office for the Prevention of Mass Atrocities.
• The Coordinating Office for the Prevention of Mass Atrocities should create standard operating procedures for disseminating intelligence concerning the risks of mass atrocities throughout the whole of government.

*Building Capacity*
• The Government of Canada should establish a Canadian Prevention Corps.
• The Government of Canada should increase its diplomatic and development presence in fragile countries.
• The Government of Canada should continue enhancing the Canadian Forces' capabilities by increasing its force strength and developing operational concepts, doctrine, force structure, and training to support civilian protection.

---

## SUMMARY RECOMMENDATIONS FOR CIVIL SOCIETY AND THE NEWS MEDIA IN THE UNITED STATES AND CANADA

*Ensuring Knowledge*
• American and Canadian civil society organizations should develop permanent domestic constituencies by forming national coalitions for the responsibility to protect in the United States and Canada.
• American and Canadian civil society organizations should expand their advocacy by targeting local/municipal and state/provincial levels of government to support the responsibility to protect.
• American and Canadian civil society groups should develop strategic, outcome-based proposals geared towards key decision makers in government.

· American and Canadian civil society groups should leverage new information and communications technologies to educate the public and government.
· American and Canadian civil society groups should initiate public discussions on the prevention of mass atrocities and related foreign policy issues.
· Individual journalists, media owners, and managers in the United States and Canada should commit themselves to "the responsibility to report."

# R2P's Stringent Criteria Limiting the Use of Force

Critics often unjustifiably single out the responsibility to protect as a doctrine that promotes the use of military force. w21 presents this appendix to communicate to policy makers and critics alike that the responsibility to protect has strict criteria for the use of force. What follows are two extracts from an information sheet prepared by the Global Centre for the Responsibility to Protect, entitled "About the Responsibility to Protect: Frequently Asked Questions," available in full at http://globalr2p.org/about/faq.html. These extracts define the criteria under which military force can be considered legitimate for humanitarian intervention and focus on the second Iraq war in light of these criteria.

*Under what circumstances would military action be considered?*
Military action offers both a threat to deter actors and, ultimately, a means to prevent or stop atrocities, but even then the failure of non-military measures would not automatically trigger a military response. There are a number of criteria that have to be satisfied, quite apart from the issue of legal authority, before such intervention could be considered legitimate. The ICISS report proposes five "precautionary principles," drawn from centuries of theory and practice in many different cultural contexts, to help guide such decisions. The first is paramount: the violence in question must be of such a serious nature, encompassing large-scale actual or threatened loss of life or ethnic cleansing, that the grave risks associated with any use of force

should be contemplated. Second, the primary purpose of the intervention must be to prevent or halt such suffering. Third, military force must be the last resort. Fourth, the means must be proportional to the ends sought. Lastly, the intervention must have a reasonable prospect of success, with the consequences of the action not being worse than the consequences of inaction. Kofi Annan's 2005 reform proposal, *In Larger Freedom*, suggests similar language.

*Doesn't the Iraq war show that R2P is really about regime change?*
No, but there can be little question that the 2003 invasion of Iraq has done real harm to the proposition that military force can be used, in extreme cases, for humanitarian ends. Neither the George W. Bush administration nor its allies sought to justify the war, and the overthrow of Saddam Hussein, chiefly as a humanitarian response to the regime's tyranny. But because some advocates of the invasion did make this claim, and others – and especially British Prime Minister Tony Blair – offered it as a retrospective rationalization, the war has at times been viewed as a kind of demonstration project of the responsibility to protect. Indeed, skeptics of R2P have been able to cite the Iraq war as "proof" that the powerful will cynically deploy the new norm to justify acts of aggression in pursuit of national interest, and in the process will cause worse violations of human rights than those they allegedly seek to remedy. The Iraq war should have no bearing on judgments about the merits of R2P. Saddam Hussein brutally violated the human rights of his people; but by 2003, he was no longer engaging in the grossest acts of ethnic cleansing, or of mass murder, that he had a decade earlier, and military action would not have satisfied either the imminence or last resort precautionary guidelines. In the run-up to the war, the United States and the United Kingdom sought to persuade the Security Council that Iraq had violated UN resolutions about weapons of mass destruction, not that it had committed atrocities against its own people.

# W2I Interview List

| | United States | |
| Name | Relevant professional positions | Interview date and location |
| --- | --- | --- |
| Bailey, Michael | Military Advisor to Presidential Special Envoy Anthony Lake, 1998–2000; Director, Post Conflict Operations, RONCO Consulting Corporation, 2003-present | 10 October 2008, Washington DC |
| Bishop, Jim | American Foreign Service Officer, 1962–95; Vice President, Humanitarian Policy and Practice, Interaction | 25 November 2008, Washington DC |
| Bushnell, Prudence | Principal Deputy Assistant Secretary for African Affairs, State Department, 1993–94 | 10 June 2008, Washington DC |
| Cohen, Herman J. | Former Assistant Secretary of State for Africa, State Department, 1989–93 | 23 December 2008, telephone interview |
| Cohen, Jared | Author of *One Hundred Days of Silence: America and the Rwanda Genocide* | 24 November 2008, Washington DC |
| Dagne, Ted | Africa Specialist, the Congressional Research Service; Assistant to Congressman Donald M. Payne (NJ) | 30 July 2008, Washington DC |
| Deng, Francis M. | Special Adviser to the United Nations Secretary-General on the Prevention of Genocide, 2007–present | 5 September 2008, New York NY |

| Name | Relevant professional positions | *Interview date and location* |
|---|---|---|
| Des Forges, Alison L. | Former Senior Advisor to the Africa Division at Human Rights Watch; author of *Leave None to Tell the Story* | 21 November 2008, telephone interview |
| Fowler, Jerry | Former founding director of the US Holocaust Memorial Museum's Committee on Conscience; President, Save Darfur, 2008–present | 8 October 2008, Washington DC |
| Hall, Tony P. | Member of US House of Representatives (Ohio), 1979–2002; US Ambassador to the UN Agencies for Food and Agriculture, 2002–06 | 12 June 2008, Washington DC |
| Halperin, Morton | Special Assistant to the President and Senior Director for Democracy, National Security Council, 1994–96; Director of Policy Planning, State Department, 1998–2001 | 9 June 2008, Washington DC |
| Hirsch, Dean R. | President and CEO, World Vision International | 6 January 2009, telephone interview |
| Holt, Victoria | Senior Associate, Henry L. Stimson Center | 7 October 2008, Washington DC |
| Levine, Iain | Program Director, Human Rights Watch | 6 May 2008, New York NY |
| Lindberg, Tod | Research Fellow, Hoover Institution, Stanford University | 10 October 2008, Washington DC |
| Lyman, Princeton N. | Assistant Secretary of State for International Organization Affairs, State Department, 1996–98 | 25 November 2008, Washington DC |
| Natsios, Andrew | Vice President, World Vision United States, 1993–97; Administrator of USAID, 2001–05; US Special Envoy for Darfur, 2006–07 | 18 November 2008, Washington DC |
| Odom, Thomas | Former US Defense Attaché to Rwanda and Zaire; author of *Journey into Darkness: Genocide in Rwanda* | 13 November 2008, telephone interview |
| Orth, Rick | Principal Defense Intelligence Agency Analyst, Department of Defense, 1994 | 13 November 2008, telephone interview |

| Name | Relevant professional positions | Interview date and location |
|---|---|---|
| Pace, William | Executive Director, World Federalist Movement-Institute for Global Policy | 7 May 2008, New York NY |
| Payne, Donald | Member of US House of Representatives (NJ), 1988-present | 30 July 2008, Washington DC |
| Rawson, David P. | US Ambassador to Rwanda, 1993–96 | 30 November 2008, Manitou Beach MI |
| Roth, Kenneth | Executive Director, Human Rights Watch, 1993–present | 6 May 2008, New York NY |
| Schultz Heim, Laurie | Senior policy advisor to Senator Jim Jeffords, 1989–2006; Director of Congressional Relations, United States Institute of Peace, 2006–present | 19 November 2008, Washington DC |
| Sewall, Sarah | Deputy Assistant Secretary for Peacekeeping and Humanitarian Assistance, the Department of Defense, 1993–2001; Director, Carr Center for Human Rights Policy, Harvard University, 2006–08 | 8 September 2008, Cambridge MA |
| Shattuck, John | Former Assistant Secretary of State for Democracy, Human Rights and Labor, State Department, 1993–98 | 1 December 2008, Boston MA |
| Smith, Gayle | Senior Advisor and Chief of Staff to the Administrator of USAID, 1994–98; Senior Fellow, Center for American Progress | 11 June 2008, Washington DC |
| Stares, Paul B. | Director, Center for Preventive Action, Council on Foreign Relations | 8 October 2008, Washington DC |
| Talbott, Strobe | Deputy Secretary of State, 1994–2001; President of the Brookings Institution | 10 June 2008, Washington DC |
| Wharton Jr., Clifton R. | Deputy Secretary of State, 1993 | 5 September 2008, New York NY |
| Williams, H. Roy | Senior official, International Rescue Committee, 1985–98; Director of Office of US Foreign Disaster Assistance, 1998–2001 | 26 November 2008, New York NY |
| Winter, Roger | Executive Director, US Committee on Refugees, 1981–2001 | 10 June 2008, Washington DC |

144

| Name | Relevant professional positions | Interview date and location |
|---|---|---|
| Wolpe, Howard | Director of the Africa Program and Leadership Project, Woodrow Wilson International Center for Scholars | 11 June 2008, Washington DC |
| Woocher, Lawrence | Senior Program Officer, Center for Conflict Analysis and Prevention, United States Institute of Peace | 10 October 2008, Washington DC |
| Anonymous | Senior official, State Department | 13 July 2008, Washington DC |
| Anonymous | Senior government official | 1 August 2008, Washington DC |

## Canada

| Name | Relevant professional positions | Interview date and location |
|---|---|---|
| Adelman, Howard | Emeritus Professor of Philosophy, York University; author of *Early Warning and Conflict Management: Joint Evaluation of Emergency Assistance to Rwanda* | 2 June 2008, Toronto ON |
| Allmand, Warren | President, the International Centre for Human Rights and Democratic Development, 1997–2002; President, World Federalist Movement-Canada, 2004-present | 22 January 2009, Montreal QC |
| Axworthy, Lloyd | Minister of Foreign Affairs, 1995–2000 | 21 July 2008, Winnipeg MB |
| Baril, Maurice | Military advisor to the UN Secretary General and head of the Military Division of the Department of Peacekeeping Operations, UN, 1992–95; Chief of the Defence Staff, 1997–2001 | 28 July 2008, Ottawa ON |
| Broadbent, Ed | Member of Parliament and Leader of the New Democratic Party, 1975–89; Director, International Centre for Human Rights and Democratic Development, 1990–96 | 6 February 2009, telephone interview |
| Calder, Kenneth J. | Assistant Deputy Minister, Policy, Department of National Defence, 1991–2006 | 4 November 2008, Ottawa ON |

145

| Name | Relevant professional positions | Interview date and location |
|------|----------------------------------|------------------------------|
| Castonguay, Jacques | Social psychologist and military historian; author of *Les Casques Bleus au Rwanda* | 21 November 2008, Montreal QC |
| Chrétien, Raymond | Secretary General of the UN's Special Envoy to the Great Lakes Region of Central Africa, 1996; Canadian Ambassador to the United States, 1994–2000 | 4 June 2008, Montreal QC |
| Collenette, David | Minister of National Defence, 1993–96 | 17 November 2008, Ottawa ON |
| Dallaire, Roméo | Force Commander, United Nations Assistance Mission in Rwanda, 1993–94 | 5 December 2008, Montreal QC |
| de Chastelain, John | Chief of the Defence Staff, 1989–93, 1994–95; Canadian Ambassador to the United States, 1994 | 12 December 2008, Ottawa ON |
| Delvoie, Louis | Former Assistant Deputy Minister, Policy, Department of National Defence | 8 July 2008, Kingston ON |
| Fowler, Robert | Deputy Minister, Department of National Defence, 1989–95; Canadian Ambassador to the UN, 1995–2000 | 24 October 2008, Ottawa ON |
| Fréchette, Louise | Canadian Ambassador to the United Nations, 1992–94; Deputy Minister of National Defence, 1995–98; Deputy Secretary General of the United Nations, 1998–2006 | 30 May 2008, Montreal QC |
| Fried, Mark | Director of Advocacy, Oxfam Canada | 20 November 2008, Ottawa ON |
| Gordon, Nancy | Director of Advocacy, CARE Canada, 1993–2005 | 4 November 2008, Ottawa ON |
| Gotlieb, Allan | Canadian Ambassador to the United States 1981–89 | 15 July 2008, Toronto ON |
| Graham, Bill | Minister of Foreign Affairs, 2002–04; Minister of National Defence, 2004–06 | 13 June 2008 and 27 November 2008, Toronto ON |
| Heinbecker, Paul | Assistant Deputy Minister, Global and Security Policy, Department of Foreign Affairs, 1996–2000; Canadian Ambassador to the United Nations, 2000–04 | 6 October 2008, Ottawa ON |

| Name | Relevant professional positions | Interview date and location |
|------|--------------------------------|-----------------------------|
| Hubert, Don | Former Director of the Human Security Division, Department of Foreign Affairs; former consultant for the International Commission on Intervention and State Sovereignty | 6 October 2008, Ottawa ON |
| Ignatieff, Michael | Director, Carr Center for Human Rights Policy, Harvard University, 2000–05; Member of Parliament and Leader of the Official Opposition, Liberal Party of Canada | 4 June 2008, Ottawa ON |
| Judd, James | Assistant Secretary to the Cabinet, Foreign and Defence Policy, Privy Council Office, 1992–94; Deputy Minister, Department of National Defence, 1998–2002 | 13 January 2009, Ottawa ON |
| Larose-Edwards, Paul | Executive Director, CANADEM | 18 December 2008, telephone interview |
| MacKenzie, Lewis | Commander, Sector Sarajevo, UNPROFOR, Yugoslavia, 1992 | 29 July 2008, Almonte ON |
| Martin, Douglas | Former General Secretary, the Bahá'í Community of Canada | 26 November 2008, Toronto ON |
| Martin, Keith | Member of Parliament, 1993-present | 21 November 2008, Ottawa ON |
| McWhinney, Edward | Member of Parliament, 1994–2000; Parliamentary Secretary to the Minister of Foreign Affairs, 1997–98 | 6 June 2008, Vancouver BC |
| Monahan, John | Executive Director, The Mosaic Institute | 13 April 2009, telephone interview |
| Ouellet, André | Secretary of State for External Affairs, 1993–95; Minister of Foreign Affairs,1995–96 | 5 November 2008, Ottawa ON |
| Pardy, Gar | Former official, Department of Foreign Affairs | 21 November 2008, Ottawa ON |
| Rae, Bob | Premier of Ontario, 1990–95; Member of Parliament and Official Foreign Affairs Critic for the Liberal Party of Canada, 2008-present | 3 June 2008, Ottawa ON |
| Sallot, Jeff | Former national security reporter for *The Globe and Mail* | 14 November 2008, Ottawa ON |

| Name | Relevant professional positions | Interview date and location |
|------|--------------------------------|-----------------------------|
| Watson, John A. | CEO, CARE Canada, 1987–2007 | 7 August 2008, Ottawa ON |
| Wright, David | Canadian Ambassador to NATO, 1997–2003 | 18 September 2008, Toronto ON |
| Anonymous | Former official, Department of Foreign Affairs | 27 November 2008, Montreal QC |
| Anonymous | Journalist in Afghanistan | 19 November 2008, telephone interview |
| Anonymous | Journalist | 21 November 2008, Ottawa ON |
| Anonymous | Official, Department of Foreign Affairs | 26 November 2008, telephone interview |

APPENDIX FOUR

# W2I Team

PROJECT CO-DIRECTORS
LIEUTENANT-GENERAL THE HONOURABLE ROMÉO A. DALLAIRE
(Ret.) had a distinguished career in the Canadian military and was appointed Assistant Deputy Minister (Human Resources) in the Department of National Defence in 1998. In 1994, General Dallaire commanded the United Nations Assistance Mission for Rwanda. His book *Shake Hands with the Devil: The Failure of Humanity in Rwanda*, was awarded the Governor General's Literary Award for Non-Fiction in 2004. Since his retirement from the military, he has written extensively about humanitarian assistance and human rights. As a fellow of the Carr Center for Human Rights Policy in the Kennedy School of Government at Harvard University, he has pursued research on conflict resolution and the use of child soldiers. He has received numerous honors and awards, including Officer of the Order of Canada in 2002, Grand Officer of the National Order of Québec in 2005, and the Aegis Award for Genocide Prevention from the Aegis Trust (United Kingdom). Canada's Governor General, Her Excellency the Right Honourable Adrienne Clarkson, presented him with the United Nations Association of Canada's Pearson Peace Medal in 2005. He was appointed to the Senate of Canada effective 24 March 2005. As a senator he is a member of the Senate Standing Committee on Human Rights and visited Darfur as a member of Prime Minister Paul Martin's Special Advisory Team on Darfur. Senator Dallaire is the Senior Fellow at the

Montreal Institute for Genocide and Human Rights Studies and a member of the United Nations Secretary General's Advisory Committee on Genocide Prevention. He is currently writing a book on child soldiers.

FRANK CHALK, Professor of History, Concordia University (Montreal, Canada) and Director, Montreal Institute for Genocide and Human Rights Studies, is co-author, with Kurt Jonassohn, of *The History and Sociology of Genocide*, an associate editor of the three-volume Macmillan Reference USA *Encyclopedia of Genocide and Crimes Against Humanity* (2004), and co-author, with Danielle Kelton, of "Mass Atrocity Crimes in Darfur and The Response of Government of Sudan Media to International Pressure," in *The World and Darfur* edited by Amanda Grzyb (2009). In 1975–76, he was a Fulbright Fellow at the University of Ibadan (Nigeria). He served as president of the International Association of Genocide Scholars (1999- 2001), and is a past president of the Canadian Association of African Studies. In 2000–01, he was a fellow at the Center for Advanced Holocaust Studies of the US Holocaust Memorial Museum in Washington DC. His current research is focused on radio broadcasting in the incitement and prevention of genocide and domestic laws of genocide.

RESEARCHERS

KYLE MATTHEWS is Lead Researcher at the Montreal Institute for Genocide and Human Rights Studies at Concordia University. He joined the Will to Intervene Project after more than five years of diplomatic service at the United Nations High Commissioner for Refugees. During that time, he was posted to the southern Caucasus (Tbilisi), the Democratic Republic of the Congo (Kinshasa) and Switzerland (Geneva). He previously worked for CARE Canada in Albania and later at its headquarters in Ottawa, where he managed various humanitarian response initiatives and peace-building projects in Afghanistan, sub-Saharan Africa and the Middle East. Originally from Ottawa, he received his BA in History from Carleton University (1996), completed his Master of Arts in Development and International Relations at Aalborg University in Denmark (2001), and earned a certificate

in Refugee Issues from York University (2002). He is a member
of the Montreal Council on Foreign Relations and vice-president
of the board of the Canadian International Council (Montreal
branch). He is also a member of the Canadian International
Council's working group on intervention and has advised members of Parliament on issues related to international peace and
security.

CARLA BARQUEIRO, researcher for the w21 Project, completed her
BA and MA in Sociology at McGill University and her PhD at the
Department of International Politics at Aberystwyth University.
Her research focuses on human security, international law, and
Canadian and American foreign policy. She is a two-time recipi-
ent of the Human Security in Cities Graduate Research Award
from Canada's Department of Foreign Affairs and International
Trade (DFAIT) and the Canadian Consortium on Human Secur-
ity. Her policy publications include *An Examination of Urban
Violent Crime in Rio de Janeiro & São Paulo* (online, DFAIT,
June, 2006) and *Children in Endemic Urban Violence: Assess-
ing the 'Protection Gap' through a Human Security Perspective*
(forthcoming, DFAIT). She currently lives in Washington DC.

SIMON DOYLE, researcher for the w21 Project and Ottawa-based
journalist, joined MIGS after more than five years of work in
journalism. As a former reporter with the CanWest News parliamentary bureau in Ottawa, and former deputy editor of *The Hill
Times* newspaper, he has written extensively about federal lobbying and Canadian politics and policy. He is a member of the
Canadian Study of Parliament Group and the Historical Society
of Ottawa, and volunteers a regular column about the news business for the Canadian Association of Journalists' *Media* magazine. He holds an MJ from Carleton University (2006) and a BA
in history from the University of Toronto (2002).

The w21 Project would like to acknowledge the work of other
researchers and interns who made valuable contributions to the
realization of this book. Richard Pilkington and Sarah Meyer
prepared a conceptual outline of a research report on the will

to intervene. Richard expertly developed a budget and funding plan for the study. Erin Jessee, Sarah Meyer, and Richard
Pilkington conducted an extensive literature review at the outset
of the W2I Project. Miriam Rabkin expertly and energetically
assisted in conducting interviews and research and coordinated
meetings with the members of the Research Steering Committee.
Julia Pettengill provided much appreciated editorial help from
afar. Robert Stewart also provided research and editorial assistance. Eugenia Zorbas assisted in the review of the French ver-
sion of the original research report. We thank Carol Berger and
Avi Goldberg for their brief service with W2I. Lastly, we would
like to thank MIGS administrator Nadav Aigen and our interns
– Abraham Pedersen, Eli Zeldin, Ryan Cronsberry, Sarah Flatto,
and Anne Marie Poitras – for their valuable contributions.

# Research Steering Committee

The w21 Project invited a distinguished group of policy makers and experts to provide strategic advice throughout its implementation. Research Steering Committee meetings took place in Montreal on 26 May 2008 and 29 September 2008. Biographies of the members of the Research Steering Committee are listed below.

MAURICE BARIL served in the Canadian Forces for forty years. During his military career, he held command and staff responsibilities across Canada and in Europe, the United States, the Middle East and Africa. In the 1990s, he was commander of the Army Combat Training Centre, military advisor to the Secretary General of the United Nations in New York, and commander of the Canadian Army from 1995–97. He was promoted to the rank of general in 1997 and appointed Canada's chief of defence staff until his retirement in 2001. He is a graduate of Canadian Army Command and Staff College, US Army Special Forces School, Canadian Forces Command and Staff College, and École Supérieure de Guerre in Paris. Since retirement, General (Ret.) Baril has been special advisor to the ambassador for mine action of the Department of Foreign Affairs Canada. In January 2003, he was appointed inspector general in the Department of Peacekeeping Operations at the UN Secretariat.

ED BROADBENT was leader of the New Democratic Party of Canada from 1975–89, as representative for Oshawa. From 1990–96,

Broadbent was the founding president of the International Centre for Human Rights and Democratic Development in Montreal. He was made a member of the Privy Council in 1982, an Officer of the Order of Canada in 1993, and a Companion of the Order of Canada in 2002. He returned to Parliament in 2004–06, as member of Parliament for Ottawa Centre. He is now a Fellow at the School of Policy Studies, Queen's University.

FRED C. FISCHER worked for the US Government for thirty-eight years, during which time he directed some of the largest disaster relief operations ever mounted. These operations included earthquake recovery in Guatemala and Nicaragua, famine and refugee relief in Pakistan, Djibouti, Kenya, southern Sudan, Somalia, Malawi, and Mozambique, covert cross-border humanitarian assistance from Pakistan into Afghanistan during the Soviet invasion, and aid to the victims of apartheid in South Africa. His overseas assignments included first secretary of the American Embassy in Bonn, Germany (1964–68), US coordinator for emergency relief in Ethiopia during the famine of 1984–86, and director of the USAID Regional Economic Development Services Office for East and Southern Africa (1990–95). He was named Federal Executive of the Year in 1986 for management of the emergency relief program in Ethiopia – the largest program of its kind ever carried out by the United States. Since retiring in 1995, he has carried out consulting assignments for USAID and the Inter-American Development Bank. He graduated from the University of Wisconsin with a BA in Journalism and Political Science in 1956 and was a Sloan Fellow at the Graduate School of Business, Stanford University, 1974–75.

TOM FLANAGAN is the award-winning author of *Harper's Team: Behind the Scenes in the Conservative Rise to Power* (2007) and *Waiting for the Wave: The Reform Party and Preston Manning* (1995). He managed Stephen Harper's campaign for the leadership of the Canadian Alliance (2002) and of the Conservative Party of Canada (2004), as well as the Conservative Party's national election campaign in 2004. He was the senior communications adviser for the Conservative Party in their successful 2006 election campaign. He studied political science at Notre Dame University, the Free University of West Berlin, and Duke University, where he received his PhD. He has taught political science at the University of Calgary since 1968 and was appointed University Professor in 2007. He was elected to the Royal Society of Canada in 1996.

ROBERT FOWLER has had a distinguished career as a Canadian diplomat and public servant. He was the prime minister's personal representative for Africa. He was a member of former prime minister Paul Martin's special advisory team on Darfur. Fowler served as Canada's ambassador to the United Nations (1995–2000) and Italy (2000–06), and as foreign policy advisor to three prime ministers. He was deputy minister of national defence from 1989–95.

YOINE GOLDSTEIN was appointed to the Senate in 2005. A graduate of the Faculty of Law at McGill University in 1958, he obtained a Doctorat de l'Université from the Université de Lyon in 1960. From 1973 to 1997, he taught law at Université de Montréal. In 2001 and 2002, he served as chair of the Federal Personal Insolvency Task Force. In 2003, he served as special advisor to the Senate Standing Committee on Banking, Trade and Commerce in connection with its report on amendments to Canadian bankruptcy and insolvency legislation. He is the only Canadian lawyer to have been elected a fellow of both the American College of Bankruptcy and the American College of Trial Lawyers. He received the Lord Reading Law Society Human Rights Award in 1992 and the Lord Reading Law Society Service Award in 1998. In 2007 he received the Quebec Bar's honorary distinction of Avocat Émérite. He is a member of the Community Advisory Board of the Concordia University Chair of Canadian Jewish Studies.

BILL GRAHAM is a former minister of Foreign Affairs and minister of National Defence. Before entering the public service and serving as a member of Parliament for over thirteen years, Graham taught in the Faculty of Law at the University of Toronto, where he pioneered the international law program. He was a member of the House of Commons Standing Committee on Foreign Affairs and International Trade from 1994–2002 and chairman from 1996–2002. In 1998, he led the drafting of the Standing Committee report on the Arctic. He served as leader of the Official Opposition in 2006 and retired from Parliament in 2007.

DAVID A. HAMBURG, MD, is DeWitt Wallace Distinguished Scholar at Weill Cornell Medical College and chairs the UN Advisory Committee on Genocide Prevention. He was president of the Carnegie Corporation of New York from 1982–97, and has been a professor at Stanford University and Harvard University. Hamburg is the author of *No More Killing Fields: Preventing Deadly Conflict* (2002) and *Learning to Live Together: Preventing Hatred and Violence in Child and Adolescent Development* (2004). He was a member of President Clinton's Defense Policy Board and the president's Committee of Advisors on Science and Technology, and was the founder of the Carnegie Commission on Science, Technology and Government. He is the recipient of the National Academy of Sciences Public Welfare Medal and the Presidential Medal of Freedom.

TED KOPPEL is Discovery Channel's managing editor. In this role, he anchors *Koppel on Discovery*, a series of long-form programming that examines major global topics and events for the largest cable network in the United States. He and his team of award-winning producers joined the network in January 2006. Koppel is also a senior news analyst for National Public Radio. Koppel came to Discovery Channel after forty-two years at ABC News. From 1980 until 2005, he was the anchor and managing editor of ABC News *Nightline*, one of the most honored broadcasts in television history. As the nation's longest running network daily news anchor, his interviews and reporting touched every significant news story over a span of twenty-five years. A member of the Broadcasting Hall of Fame, Koppel has won every major broadcasting award including forty-two Emmy awards (one for lifetime achievement), eight George Foster Peabody awards, ten

DuPont-Columbia awards and two George Polk awards. His ten Overseas Press Club awards make him the most honored journalist in the club's history. He has received more than twenty honorary degrees from universities in the United States.

JUAN É. MÉNDEZ was the United Nations' Special Advisor on the Prevention of Genocide from 2004–07. He has taught at the University of Notre Dame, Georgetown University Law Center, the Johns Hopkins School of Advanced International Studies, and in the Oxford Master's Programme in International Human Rights Law. His work on behalf of political prisoners of Argentina's military dictatorship in the 1970s led to his torture and administrative detention for over a year, during which time Amnesty International adopted him as a "prisoner of conscience." Following his release, he moved to the United States and began work with Human Rights Watch. Méndez has received multiple awards for his work, including the University of Dayton's inaugural Oscar A. Romero Award for Leadership in Service to Human Rights (2000) and the Jeanne and Joseph Sullivan Award of the Heartland Alliance (2003).

ALEX NEVE is Secretary General of Amnesty International Canada's English-speaking branch. He has participated in Amnesty International missions to Burundi, Chad, Colombia, Côte d'Ivoïre, Guinea, Honduras, South Africa, Zimbabwe, and Grassy Narrows, Ontario. He represented Amnesty International at the 2001 Summit of the Americas, the 2002 G8 Summit, and the 2003 Asian Plurilateral Symposium on Human Rights in China. He has appeared before numerous Canadian parliamentary committees as well as various UN and Inter-American human rights bodies. He holds a Bachelor of Commerce and Bachelor of Laws from Dalhousie University, and a Master's degree in international human rights law from the University of Essex. Neve is chair of the Board of Directors of the Canadian Centre for International Justice, and a member of the Board of Directors of Partnership Africa Canada. He was named a Trudeau Foundation Mentor in 2007 and is an officer of the Order of Canada.

ANDRÉ PRATTE is the editor-in-chief of Montreal's *La Presse* newspaper and the author of five books on journalism and politics, including *Aux pays des merveilles: Essai sur les mythes politiques québécois* (2006), *Le Temps des girouettes* (2003) and *L'Énigme Charest* (1997), a biography of Quebec premier Jean Charest. He was one of twelve prominent Quebecers, led by former premier Lucien Bouchard, who signed the 2005 manifesto entitled "Pour un Québec lucide" ("For a Clear-Eyed Vision of Quebec"), which provoked a passionate debate about Quebec's future. He edited and contributed to *Reconquérir le Canada: un nouveau projet pour la nation Québécoise* (*Reconquering Canada: A New Project for the Quebec Nation*), a collection of essays promoting federalism in the province.

KENNETH PREWITT is the Carnegie Professor of Public Affairs at the School of International and Public Affairs at Columbia University. His previous positions include director of the US Census Bureau (1998–2001), director of the National Opinion Research Center, president of the Social Science Research Council and senior vice-president of the Rockefeller Foundation. He is a fellow of the American Academy of Arts and Sciences, the American Academy of Political and Social Science, the American Association for the Advancement of Science, the Center for Advanced Study in the Behavioral Sciences, and the Russell-Sage Foundation, and is a member of other professional associations, including the Council on Foreign Relations. Among his awards are a Guggenheim fellowship, honorary degrees from Carnegie Mellon University and Southern Methodist University, a Distinguished Service Award from the New School for Social Research, and various awards associated with his directorship of the Census Bureau. In 1990 he was awarded the Officer's Cross of the Order of Merit from the Federal Republic of Germany.

DAVID SCHEFFER is the Mayer Brown/Robert A. Helman Professor of Law and director of the Center for International Human Rights at Northwestern University School of Law, where he teaches international criminal law and international human rights law. He is the former US ambassador-at-large for war crimes issues (1997–2001) and led the US delegation in the negotiations leading to the establishment of the International Criminal Court. During the first term of the Clinton Administration, he was senior advisor and counsel to US Permanent Representative to the United Nations Madeleine Albright, and served on the Deputies Committee of the National Security Council.

HUGH D. SEGAL spent several decades in the private and public sector before being appointed to the Senate of Canada in 2005. His public sector experience spans the Cabinet office at Queen's Park and the prime minister's office in Ottawa. Since his appointment to the Senate, he has sat on the Senate Foreign Affairs and International Trade Committee, the Agriculture and Forestry Committee, the Aboriginal Affairs and Northern Development Committee, and the Special Committee on Anti-Terrorism. He is a former president of the Institute for Research on Public Policy, where he remains a senior fellow, and also teaches at Queen's University. He sits on various corporate and public boards, as well as the boards of not-for-profit and charitable organizations. In 2003, he was named to the Order of Canada. In 2004, he was awarded an honorary doctorate from the Royal Military College and, in 2005, was appointed an honorary captain of the Canadian navy. He has authored numerous books and articles on public policy and the Conservative Party. Before his Senate appointment, he was a regular television commentator on the CTV, PBS, and CBC networks.

JENNIFER ALLEN SIMONS is president of The Simons Foundation, Visiting Fellow at the Morris J. Wosk Centre for Dialogue and adjunct professor in the School for International Studies at Simon Fraser University. She is a former director and adjunct professor of the Simons Centre for Disarmament and Non-Proliferation Research at the Liu Institute for Global Issues, University of British Columbia, which she established jointly with the university. She was a member of the Canadian government delegation to the UN 2000 Non-Proliferation Treaty Review Conference and the 2002 Non-Proliferation Treaty Conference, and is a member

of the Steering Committee of the Canadian Department of Foreign Affairs/Non-Governmental Organizations Consultations
on Nuclear Issues. Simon Fraser University honored her with
the Jennifer Allen Simons Chair in Liberal Studies and the 1996
Chancellor's Distinguished Service Award. She was awarded Her
Majesty Queen Elizabeth II's Golden Jubilee Commemorative
Medal for service in support of the global effort to eradicate
land mines and is a recipient of the 2006 Vancouver Citizens'
Peace Award.

JANICE GROSS STEIN is the Belzberg Professor of Conflict
Management in the department of Political Science and director of the Munk Centre for International Studies at the University of Toronto. She is the co-author with Eugene Lang of *The
Unexpected War: Canada in Kandahar*, which was awarded
the 2007 Shaughnessy Cohen Prize for Political Writing. Her
other books include *Networks of Knowledge: Innovation in
International Learning* (2000), *The Cult of Efficiency* (2001),
and *Street Protests and Fantasy Parks* (2001). In 2006, she was
awarded an honorary doctorate of laws by the University of
Alberta and by the University of Cape Breton. She was the Mas-
sey Lecturer in 2001 and a Trudeau Fellow in 2003. Gross Stein
is the recipient of the Molson Prize by the Canada Council for
an outstanding contribution by a social scientist to public debate
and an honorary foreign member of the American Academy of
Arts and Sciences. She is a fellow of the Royal Society of Canada
and a member of the Order of Canada and the Order of Ontario.

ALLAN THOMPSON is an assistant professor at Carleton University's School of Journalism and Communication. He joined
the faculty in 2003 after seventeen years as a reporter with the
*Toronto Star*, Canada's largest circulation daily newspaper.
Thompson worked for ten years as a correspondent for the *Star*
on Parliament Hill, reporting on foreign affairs, defense and
immigration issues. He first reported from Rwanda for the *Star*
in 1996 during the mass exodus of Rwandan refugees from eastern Zaire. He visited Rwanda again in 1998 to research a series
of feature articles. Over the years he has also chronicled Roméo

Dallaire's career in a series of reports for the *Star*. In January 2004, Thompson travelled to Arusha, Tanzania, to report on Dallaire's testimony before the International Criminal Tribunal for Rwanda.

THOMAS G. WEISS is Presidential Professor of Political Science at The City University of New York (CUNY) Graduate Center and director of the Ralph Bunche Institute for International Studies, where he is co-director of the United Nations Intellectual History Project. Weiss has served as the interim executive director of the Global Centre for the Responsibility to Protect. He was awarded the Grand Prix Humanitaire de France in 2006 and is chair of the Academic Council on the UN System. He was a co-editor of *Global Governance*, research director of the International Commission on Intervention and State Sovereignty, research professor at Brown University's Watson Institute for International Studies, executive director of the Academic Council on the UN System and of the International Peace Academy, a member of the UN Secretariat, and a consultant to several public and private agencies. He has written or edited some thirty-five books and numerous scholarly articles about multilateral approaches to international peace and security, humanitarian action, and sustainable development.

HARVEY YAROSKY has practiced law in Montreal since 1962 and has been a member and chair of various committees of the Bar of Montréal, the Bar of Québec and the Canadian Bar association, relating to the administration of justice. He taught criminal law at McGill University, where he was adjunct professor of criminal law, and at the University of Ottawa and Université de Montréal. Yarosky is a fellow of the American College of Trial Lawyers and has acted as independent counsel to the Canadian Judicial Council. Yarosky was executive assistant to the Department of Justice Committee on Hate Propaganda, the report of which formed the basis of the provisions in the Canadian Criminal Code against the promotion of genocide and hate propaganda. He has served as counsel to Senator and Lt. Gen. (Ret.) Roméo Dallaire in a number of international investigations, inquiries, and proceedings regarding the 1994 Rwandan Genocide.

# Academic Consultation Group

The W21 Project invited a group of outstanding academics and experts to advise and guide the researchers. The Academic Consultation Group met in Montreal on 14 April 2008 and 10 November 2008. Biographies of the members of the Academic Consultation Group appear below.

ELIZABETH BLOODGOOD is an assistant professor of political science at Concordia University. She earned her PhD at Princeton University. Her research focuses on NGOs and their use of informational lobbying and protest tactics to influence national decision makers regarding foreign policy and international regimes. In her past work, she has examined the activities of Greenpeace, the International Campaign to Ban Landmines, Friends of the Earth, and Abolition 2000. In order to address questions about the influence of NGOs in foreign policy making, she has surveyed decision makers about their relations with NGOs and interviewed NGO staffers about their tactics and goals in both London and Washington.

DAVID CARMENT is a professor of international affairs at the Norman Paterson School of International Affairs at Carleton University and fellow of the Canadian Defence and Foreign Affairs Institute. He is a NATO Fellow and listed in *Who's Who in International Affairs*. In addition, Carment serves as the principal investigator for the Country Indicators for Foreign Policy project.

He has served as director of the Centre for Security and Defence Studies at Carleton University and is the recipient of a Carleton Graduate Students' teaching excellence award, fellowships and research awards from the Social Sciences and Humanities Research Council, Carleton University's research achievement award, and a Petro-Canada Young Innovator Award. Carment has held fellowships at Harvard University's Kennedy School of Government and at the Hoover Institution, Stanford University.

DON HUBERT led policy development on Canada's human security agenda within the Department of Foreign Affairs for nearly a decade. He has been responsible for specific initiatives on small arms proliferation, diamonds and other resources linked to armed conflict, the responsibility to protect, and corporate social responsibility. Most recently, he was director of the Human Security Division, with previous positions in Policy Planning, as coordinator of Humanitarian Affairs, and as deputy to the chair of the Kimberley Process. He has held post-doctoral positions at the Centre for Foreign Policy Studies at Dalhousie University and the Humanitarianism and War Project at Brown University, was a consultant for the International Commission on Intervention and State Sovereignty, and has taught at the School of International Affairs at Carleton University.

MICHAEL IGNATIEFF was born and raised in Toronto and earned his PhD from Harvard University, where he taught from 2000–05. He is considered one of the world's leading experts in democracy, human rights, security, and international affairs. He has advised governments and world leaders on these questions and has served on the International Commission on Kosovo and the International Commission on Intervention and State Sovereignty. He has been a regular commentator, critic, and broadcaster on television and radio in Canada, England, and the United States. As a journalist, he covered the Balkan wars for the BBC, *The Observer* and *The New Yorker*, reporting from Bosnia, Kosovo, Rwanda, Angola, and Afghanistan. On television, he has hosted many programs for the BBC, PBS, and CBC, including the award-winning 1993 series *Blood and Belonging: Journeys into the*

*New Nationalism*. In January 2006, he was elected member of Parliament for Etobicoke-Lakeshore. He is the current leader of the Liberal Party and of the Official Opposition in the Parliament of Canada.

BRUCE JENTLESON is a professor of public policy and political science at Duke University, where he served from 2000–05 as director of the Terry Sanford Institute of Public Policy. He is a leading expert on a wide range of issues in American foreign policy, with a distinguished professorial record and extensive policy experience. In 2006–07, he was a visiting senior research fellow at Oxford University and at the International Institute for Strategic Studies (London), and was a Fulbright senior research scholar in Spain. He has published numerous articles and seven books, including *American Foreign Policy: The Dynamics of Choice in the 21st Century* (3rd edition, 2007) and *Opportunities Missed, Opportunities Seized: Preventive Diplomacy in the Post-Cold War World*, a project of the Carnegie Commission on Preventing Deadly Conflict (1999). Forthcoming books – *After Bush: Getting Global Leadership Right*, *First Principles: Force and Diplomacy in the Contemporary Era*, and *Profiles in Statesmanship*, are in preparation.

PAUL KORING is a staff correspondent in *The Globe and Mail*'s Washington Bureau and specializes in international security affairs and foreign policy. He has been a foreign correspondent for *The Globe and Mail* and other news organizations since 1980 and has spent significant time covering conflicts and international security and defense issues. His "on-the-ground" conflict coverage includes the Iran-Iraq war, the Palestinian intifada, Northern Ireland, the first Gulf War, and the Balkan wars in Slovenia, Croatia, Bosnia, and Kosovo. He has made four trips to Afghanistan and has covered Canadian military overseas deployments in Haiti, Baghdad, Cyprus, and Kandahar.

MICHAEL LIPSON is an associate professor in the Department of Political Science at Concordia University. His current research addresses international organizations concerned with threats to international peace and security, focusing on non-proliferation and international peacekeeping.

STEPHEN SAIDEMAN is Canada Research Chair in International Security and Ethnic Conflict and associate professor of political science at McGill University. He has published articles on the international relations and comparative politics of ethnic conflict in a variety of journals and edited volumes. Saideman spent a year on the US Joint Staff working in the Strategic Planning and Policy Directorate on Balkans issues as part of a Council on Foreign Relations International Affairs Fellowship.

ABBY STODDARD is a policy analyst in international humanitarian affairs, conducting independent and commissioned research in association with New York University's Center on International Cooperation and the UK-based Overseas Development Institute. She is a founding member of Humanitarian Outcomes, an independent research team that provides evidence-based analysis to governments and international organizations on improving humanitarian response. Her prior work as an aid practitioner throughout the 1990s spanned such crises as Rwanda and the former Yugoslavia. Stoddard is the author of *Humanitarian Alert: NGO Information and its Impact on US Foreign Policy* (2006).

SCOTT STRAUS is an associate professor of political science and international studies at the University of Wisconsin-Madison, where he teaches classes on genocide, violence, human rights, and African politics. His book on the Rwandan Genocide, *The Order of Genocide: Race, Power, and War in Rwanda* (2006) won the 2006 Award for Excellence in Political Science and Government from the Professional and Scholarly Publishing Division of the Association of American Publishers. He has published articles relating to genocide in *Foreign Affairs*, *World Politics*, *Politics & Society*, and *Genocide Studies and Prevention*. Before entering academia, he was a freelance journalist based in Nairobi, Kenya.

AMANDA SUSSMAN has an extensive background in advocacy work with organizations such as Human Rights Watch and Greenpeace. She has been a policy adviser on human rights and refugee issues to senior Cabinet ministers in the Canadian government. She holds an MA in international affairs and economics from the Johns Hopkins University School of Advanced International Studies. Her published works include *The Art of the Possible: A Handbook for Political Activism* (2007).

ALLAN THOMPSON. See Appendix 5 (Research Steering Committee).

THOMAS G. WEISS. See Appendix 5 (Research Steering Committee).

# Notes

1 Uvin, *Aiding Violence*, 13–18.
2 Des Forges, *Leave None to Tell the Story*, 39.
3 Ibid., 38–40.
4 Kiernan, *Blood and Soil*, 555–8.
5 Otunnu, "Rwandan Refugees and Immigrants in Uganda," in Adelman and Suhrke, eds., *The Path of a Genocide*, 16.
6 Des Forges, *Leave None to Tell the Story*, 31–64.
7 Jones, "Rwanda," in Berdal and Economides, eds., *United Nations Interventionism: 1991–2004*, 135.
8 Ibid., 146–52.
9 Roméo Dallaire, W21 interview, Montreal QC, 5 December 2008.
10 Senior government official, W21 interview, Washington DC, 1 August 2008.
11 Senior government official, W21 interview.
12 Cohen, *One Hundred Days of Silence*, 17–19.
13 Herman J. Cohen, W21 interview, Washington DC, 23 December 2008.
14 UNAMIR I was created by Resolution 872 and approved by the UNSC on 6 January 1993 for a Chapter VI operation with a 2,548 troop allotment but only began deployment in October 1993.
15 Prudence Bushnell, W21 interview, Washington DC, 10 June 2008.
16 Jared Cohen, W21 interview, Washington DC, 24 November 2008.
17 Cohen, *One Hundred Days of Silence*, 176.
18 PBS Frontline Interview, "Ghosts of Rwanda," with US Assistant Secretary of State for African Affairs George Moose, 21 November 2003.

19  Bushnell, w21 interview.

20  Ibid.

21  Ibid.

22  Ibid.

23  PBS Frontline Interview, "Ghosts of Rwanda," with US Ambassador David P. Rawson, 5 October 2003.

24  For a comprehensive overview of US decision making on Somalia, see Richard A. Clarke, *Your Government Failed You: Breaking the Cycle of National Security Disasters* (New York: Harper Collins 2008).

25  Sarah Sewall, w21 interview, Cambridge, MA, 8 September 2008.

26  Ibid.

27  Ibid.

28  Cohen, *One Hundred Days of Silence*, 49–54.

29  PBS Frontline Interview, "The Triumph of Evil," with James Woods, January 1999.

30  PBS Frontline Interview, "Ghosts of Rwanda," with US National Security Advisor Anthony Lake, 15 December 2003.

31  Ibid.

32  Bushnell, w21 interview.

33  Rwandans working at the American Embassy translated the hate propaganda for US Ambassador David P. Rawson and other American diplomats. See Cohen, *One Hundred Days of Silence*, 35–7.

34  PBS Frontline Interview, "Ghosts of Rwanda," with David P. Rawson.

35  David P. Rawson, w21 interview, Manitou Beach, MI, 20 November 2008.

36  PBS Frontline Interview, "The Triumph of Evil," with former US State Department Military Advisor Tony Marley, January 1999.

37  PBS Frontline Interview, "The Triumph of Evil," with Tony Marley.

38  Bushnell, w21 interview.

39  Ibid.

40  John Shattuck, w21 interview, Boston, MA, 1 December 2008.

41  Ibid.

42  Cohen, *One Hundred Days of Silence*, 72–94.

43  Bushnell, w21 interview.

44  See Confidential State Department memorandum outlining the creation of the twenty-four-hour working group to receive all information on the situation in Rwanda, headed by Prudence Bushnell. US

Secretary of State memorandum to all diplomatic and consular posts immediate, "Working Group Formation to Deal with the Situation in Kigali and Bujumbura," 8 April 1994.

45 Bushnell, w21 interview.

46 Cohen, *One Hundred Days of Silence*, 71–80.

47 Executive Secretariat of the Operations Center at the US State Department to all state bureaus and offices, "Confidential Situation Report No.6," 8 April 1994.

48 US Central Intelligence Agency, "National Intelligence Daily," 8 April 1994.

49 Des Forges, w21 interview, Buffalo NY, 21 November 2008.

50 Rawson, w21 interview.

51 Ibid.

52 Ibid.

53 Executive Secretariat of the Operations Center at the US State Department, "Confidential Situation Report No.6," 8 April 1994.

54 Douglas Bennet, US Department of State to Secretary of State Warren Christopher, State Department Briefing Memorandum, "Phone Call to UN Secretary General Boutros-Ghali on Bosnia and Rwanda," 13 April 1994.

55 Ibid.

56 Ibid.

57 US Secretary of State Warren Christopher to US Mission USUN New York, memorandum, "Talking Points on UNAMIR withdrawal," 15 April 1994.

58 Alison Des Forges, w21 interview, Buffalo, NY, 21 November 2008.

59 Ibid.

60 Ibid.

61 Ibid.

62 Ibid.

63 Kenneth Roth, w21 interview, New York, NY, 6 May 2008.

64 PBS Frontline Interview, "Ghosts of Rwanda," with US Ambassador to the United Nations Madeleine Albright, 25 February 2004.

65 Ibid.

66 Ibid.

67 Ibid.

68 Roger Winter, w21 interview, Washington DC, 10 June 2008.

69 Ibid.

70 Ibid.

71 Copson, *The Congressional Black Caucus and Foreign Policy*, 34.

72 Ibid.

73 Ibid.

74 Ibid.

75 Power, *A Problem from Hell*, 376–7.

76 Laurie Schultz Heim, W21 interview, Washington DC, 19 November 2008.

77 Ibid.

78 US Undersecretary of Defense to the Deputy Assistant to the President for National Security Affairs, National Security Council memorandum, "Rwanda: Jamming Civilian Radio Broadcasts," 5 May 1994.

79 Ibid.

80 J. Cohen, W21 interview.

81 Des Forges, "Call to Genocide," in Thompson, ed., *The Media and the Rwanda Genocide*, 52.

82 Ibid., 41–54.

83 Tony Marley, Frank Chalk interview, 20 April 1995.

84 Ibid.

85 Livingston and Eachus, "Rwanda," in Adelman and Suhrke, eds., *The Path of a Genocide*, 210.

86 Power, *A Problem from Hell*, 356–7.

87 Cohen, *One Hundred Days of Silence*, 66–9.

88 Kuperman, "How the Media Missed the Rwanda Genocide," in Thompson, ed., *The Media and the Rwanda Genocide*, 258.

89 Ron Allen cited in Livingston and Eachus, "Rwanda," 218.

90 Roméo Dallaire, W21 interview, Montreal, QC, 5 December 2008.

91 Ibid.

92 Livingston and Eachus, "Rwanda," in Adelman and Suhrke, eds., *The Path of a Genocide*, 226–7.

93 Ibid.

94 Ibid.

95 Ibid.

96 Rick Orth, W21 interview, via telephone, 13 November 2008.

97 Shattuck, W21 interview.

98 Cohen, *One Hundred Days of Silence*, 135–7.

99 Office of the US Secretary of Defense, "Secret Discussion Paper, subject: 'Rwanda,' May 1, 1994," quoted in Power, *A Problem from Hell*, 359.

100 US Defense Intelligence Agency, Secret Defense Intelligence Report, "Rwanda: The Rwandan Patriotic Front's Offensive," 9 May 1994.

101 Des Forges, *Leave None to Tell the Story*, 225–62.

102 Orth, w21 interview.

103 Ibid.

104 Douglas J. Bennet, George C. Moose, Conrad K. Harper and John Shattuck, US Department of State, to US Secretary of the State Department, memorandum, "Has Genocide Occurred in Rwanda?" 5 May 1994.

105 Ibid.

106 Ibid.

107 Power, *A Problem from Hell*, 362.

108 Warren Christopher, US Secretary of State, to USUN and US Embassies, cable, "UN Human Rights Commission: 'Genocide' at Special Session on Rwanda," 24 May 1994, quoted in Power, *A Problem from Hell*, 362.

109 Michael R. Gordon, "U.S. to Supply 60 Vehicles for UN Troops in Rwanda," *The New York Times*, 16 June 1994, quoted in Power, *A Problem from Hell*, 363–4.

110 J. Cohen, w21 interview.

111 Ibid.

112 Barnett, *Eyewitness to Genocide*, 141–3.

113 Ibid.

114 Ibid., 150–2.

115 Power, *A Problem from Hell*, 381.

116 Dallaire, W21 Interview.

117 Mennecke and Markusen, "Genocide in Bosnia and Herzegovina," in Totten and Parsons, eds., *Century of Genocide*, 421.

118 Ibid.

119 Independent International Commission on Kosovo, *The Kosovo Report*, 41.

120 Mennecke and Markusen, "Genocide in Bosnia and Herzegovina," 419.

121 Mennecke, "Genocide in Kosovo?," in Totten and Parsons, eds., *Century of Genocide*, 450.

122 Shattuck, *Freedom on Fire*, 218.

123 Ibid. Shattuck's comment on the "erroneous" nature of Milosevic's belief that he could afford to start another war was based on his claim that Milosevic concluded that his acts of ethnic cleansing in Bosnia had come with no repercussion, such as prosecution. Rather, Milosevic had been included in the Dayton Accord negotiations, signaling to him that sparking another ethnically driven offensive carried little risk.

124 Shattuck, *Freedom on Fire*, 210.

125 Ibid.

126 Paul Heinbecker, w21 interview, Ottawa, ON, 6 October 2008.

127 Ibid.

128 Ibid.

129 Ibid.

130 H. Roy Williams, w21 interview, New York, NY, 26 November 2008.

131 4,000 of the proposed 20,000 UN peacekeepers were to be American.

132 Power, *A Problem from Hell*, 447–8.

133 Shattuck, w21 interview.

134 Morton Halperin, w21 interview, Washington DC, 9 June 2008.

135 Ibid.

136 Ibid.

137 Ibid.

138 Ibid.

139 Halperin, "Winning the Peace," in Buckley, ed., *Kosovo*, 226–7.

140 Ibid.

141 Ibid.

142 United Nations Security Council, S/Res/1199, UN Security Council 3930th meeting, 23 September 1998.

143 Economides, "Kosovo," in Berdal and Economides, eds., *United Nations Interventionism*, 217–45.

144 Egan, "The Kosovo Intervention and Collective Self-Defense," 39–58.

145 Strobe Talbott, w21 interview, Washington DC, 6 June 2008.

146 Ibid.

147 Ibid.

148 Walzer, "Kosovo," in Buckley, ed., *Kosovo*, 333–5.

149 Luttwak, "Give War a Chance," in Buckley, ed., *Kosovo*, 353.

150 Samantha Power, w21 interview, New York, NY, 6 May 2008.

151 Power, *A Problem from Hell*, 455.

152  Ackerman and Naureckas, "Following Washington's Script," in
     Hammond and Herman, eds., *Degraded Capability*, 101.
153  Ibid., 99.
154  Ibid., 100.
155  Ibid., 108.
156  Herman and Peterson, "CNN: Selling NATO's War Globally," in Ham-
     mond and Herman, eds., *Degraded Capability*, 113.
157  Johnstone, "NATO and the New World Order: Ideals and Self-Inter-
     est," in Hammond and Herman, eds., *Degraded Capability*, 7.
158  See Fron Nazi, "Balkan Diaspora I" and Nick Vucinich, "Balkan
     Diaspora II," in Buckley, ed., *Kosovo*.
159  US Department of State, "Report on the Visit of Ambassador Scheffer
     to the Border between the Former Republic of Macedonia and
     Kosovo, April 1–2 and Refugee Accounts of Atrocities," 7 April 1999.
160  Ibid.
161  Power, *A Problem from Hell*, 464–5.
162  Kenneth Roth, W21 interview, New York, NY, 6 May 2008.
163  Dykstra, "Rwanda: Tracing the Roots of Genocide," 24.
164  Gendron, *Towards a Francophone Community*, 82–98.
165  Adelman, "Canadian Policy in Rwanda," in Adelman and Suhrke,
     eds., *The Path of a Genocide*, 189.
166  The full title of the Commission was the "International Commission
     of Inquiry into Human Rights Abuses in Rwanda Since October 1st
     1990."
167  Schabas, *Genocide in International Law*, ix-xi.
168  Ed Broadbent, W21 interview, Ottawa, ON, 6 February 2009; Inter-
     national Centre for Human Rights and Democratic Development
     press release, "The Government and Armed Forces Responsible for
     the Reign of Terror in Rwanda," 8 March 1993.
169  Adelman, "Canadian Policy in Rwanda," in Adelman and Suhrke,
     eds., *The Path of a Genocide*, 191–6; André Ouellet, W21 interview,
     Ottawa, ON, 5 November 2008.
170  Robert Fowler, W21 interview, Ottawa, ON, 24 October 2008.
171  Ibid.
172  Ibid.
173  Kenneth J. Calder, W21 interview, Ottawa, ON, 4 November 2008;
     Ouellet, W21 interview.
174  Calder, W21 interview.

175  Ibid.

176  Fowler, w21 interview.

177  Former Foreign Affairs official, w21 interview, Montreal, QC, 27 November 2008.

178  Fowler, w21 interview.

179  Louise Fréchette, w21 interview, Montreal, QC, 30 May 2008.

180  Ibid.

181  Ouellet, w21 interview.

182  Ibid. This notion is also supported by Calder, w21 interview, and former Foreign Affairs official, w21 interview.

183  Calder, w21 interview.

184  Similar opposition to providing resources had emerged in 1993 when Dallaire requested additional Canadian officers for his mission. Fowler pushed for the officers despite resistance from the Canadian Forces. Calder, w21 interview; former Foreign Affairs official, w21 interview; Foreign Affairs official, w21 interview, Montreal, QC, 26 November 2008.

185  Dallaire, w21 interview.

186  Ibid.

187  Ibid.

188  Foreign Affairs official, w21 interview.

189  Former Foreign Affairs official, w21 interview; Gar Pardy, w21 interview, Ottawa, ON, 21 November 2008.

190  Fréchette, w21 interview.

191  Foreign Affairs official, w21 interview; former Foreign Affairs official, w21 interview.

192  Fréchette, w21 interview.

193  Former Foreign Affairs official, w21 interview.

194  During the month of April 1994, the *Ottawa Citizen, Toronto Star, The Globe and Mail,* and *La Presse* show no record of Ouellet's position toward the UNAMIR mission.

195  Foreign Affairs official, w21 interview.

196  Maurice Baril, w21 interview, Ottawa, ON, 24 July 2008.

197  This is in the opinion of Maurice Baril, w21 Interview.

198  Fréchette, w21 interview.

199  Allan Thompson, "Africans best for mediation, Ouellet says," *Toronto Star,* 3 May 1994.

200 US Embassy, Ottawa, to US Secretary of State, cable, "The Rwanda Crisis and Canada," 13 May 1994.

201 Ibid.

202 Foreign Affairs official, w21 interview.

203 Pardy, w21 interview.

204 Nancy Gordon, w21 interview, Ottawa, ON, 4 November 2008.

205 Ibid.

206 David Collenette, w21 interview, Ottawa, ON, 17 November 2008.

207 Ouellet, w21 interview.

208 Ibid.

209 Bartleman, *Rollercoaster*, 175.

210 Kimonyo, "Rwanda: Ottawa est prié de s'impliquer á fond dans la lutte aux 'criminels de Kigali,'" *La Presse*, 19 April 1994.

211 United Nations Security Council Resolution 912, adopted 21 April 1994.

212 Cohen, *One Hundred Days of Silence*, 187–8.

213 Ibid., 187.

214 Keith Martin, w21 interview, Ottawa, ON, 21 November 2008.

215 Canada, House of Commons Oral Question Period, 5 May 1994, 35th Parl. 1st Sess., Deb. 64, Journ. 64 (MP Lucien Bouchard, Leader of the Opposition).

216 US Embassy, Ottawa, to US Secretary of State, cable, "The Rwanda Crisis and Canada," 13 May 1994.

217 Canada, House of Commons Oral Question Period, 10 May 1994, 35th Parl. 1st Sess., Deb. 67, Journ. 67 (MP Lucien Bouchard, leader of the Opposition).

218 Dallaire, w21 interview.

219 Ibid.

220 Calder, w21 interview.

221 Calder, w21 interview; Ouellet, w21 interview.

222 Kuperman, "How the Media Missed the Rwanda Genocide," and Melvern, "Missing the Story: The Media and the Rwanda Genocide," in Thompson, ed., *The Media and the Rwanda Genocide*.

223 Livingston and Eachus, "Rwanda," in Adelman and Suhrke, eds., *The Path of a Genocide*, 226–7.

224 Jeff Sallot, w21 interview, Ottawa, ON, 14 November 2008.

225 Ibid.

226 John Watson, w21 interview, Ottawa, ON, 7 August 2008.
227 Sallot, w21 interview. For similar views at the BBC see Tom Giles, "Media Failure Over Rwanda's Genocide," and Lindsey Hilsum, "Reporting Rwanda: the Media and the Aid Agencies," in Thompson, ed., *The Media and the Rwanda Genocide.*
228 Winter, w21 interview; Winter, "Power, Not Tribalism, Stokes Rwanda's Slaughter," *The Globe and Mail,* 14 April 1994.
229 Bartleman, *Rollercoaster,* 175.
230 Bartleman, *Rollercoaster,* 175–7; Castonguay, *Les Casques bleus au Rwanda,* 155–6.
231 Dallaire, w21 interview.
232 Ibid.
233 Baril, w21 interview.
234 Dallaire, w21 interview.
235 Baril, w21 interview.
236 Ibid.
237 Ibid.
238 Fowler, w21 interview.
239 Robert Fowler, Memorandum to the minister of national defence David Collenette, 6 June 1994.
240 Ibid.
241 The memo noted the deployment of 33,000 UN troops to the former Yugoslavia and only 450 UN troops to Rwanda, while "Rwanda has suffered more killed (possibly many times more) in 2 months than Bosnia in 2 years."
242 Fowler, w21 interview.
243 Ibid.
244 Bartleman, *Rollercoaster,* 176–7.
245 Fowler, w21 interview.
246 Adelman, "Canadian Policy in Rwanda," in Adelman and Suhrke, eds., *The Path of a Genocide,* 199.
247 Dallaire, w21 interview.
248 Martin, w21 interview.
249 Collenette, w21 interview.
250 Ibid.
251 Bill Graham, w21 interview, Toronto, ON, 13 June 2008.
252 Art Eggleton, w21 interview, Ottawa, ON, 3 June 2008.
253 Fréchette, w21 interview.

254 Collenette, w21 interview.

255 Ibid.

256 Department of Foreign Affairs and International Trade, *Freedom from Fear.*

257 Graham, w21 interview.

258 Ibid.

259 Ibid.

260 Calder, w21 interview.

261 Graham, w21 interview.

262 Ibid.

263 Fowler, w21 interview.

264 David Wright, w21 interview, Toronto, ON, 18 September 2008.

265 Ibid.

266 Collenette, w21 interview.

267 Ibid.

268 Ibid.

269 Ibid.

270 Wright, "Kosovo: Inside the North Atlantic Council," in Haglund, ed., *New NATO, New Century,* viii.

271 United Nations Security Council, S/Res/1199, UN Security Council 3930th meeting, 23 September 1998

272 Independent International Commission on Kosovo, *The Kosovo Report,* 148.

273 Fowler, w21 interview.

274 Ibid.

275 It was expected that Russia would veto the resolution with support from China. Wright, "Kosovo: Inside the North Atlantic Council," in Haglund, ed., *New NATO, New Century,* xi; Heinbecker, w21 interview.

276 Fowler, w21 interview.

277 Ibid.

278 Heinbecker, w21 interview.

279 Ibid.

280 Ibid.

281 Ibid.

282 Ibid.

283 Heinbecker, w21 interview; former Department of National Defence official, w21 interview.

284  Heinbecker, w21 interview.
285  Former Department of National Defence official, w21 interview.
286  Adelman, w21 interview.
287  Wright, w21 interview.
288  Fréchette, w21 interview.
289  Eggleton, w21 interview.
290  Ibid.
291  Heinbecker, w21 interview.
292  Adelman, w21 interview.
293  Ibid.
294  The Contact Group was comprised of representatives from the United States, the United Kingdom, France, Italy, and Russia.
295  Wright, w21 interview.
296  Eggleton, w21 interview.
297  Ibid.
298  Calder, w21 interview.
299  Ibid.
300  Ibid.
301  Ibid.
302  Fowler, w21 interview.
303  Haglund and Sens, "Kosovo and the Case of the (Not So) Free Riders," in Albrecht Schnabel and Ramesh Thakur, eds., *Kosovo and the Challenge of Humanitarian Intervention* (Tokyo: United Nations University Press 2000), 181–200.
304  Heinbecker, w21 interview.
305  Canadian Press, "Canada to Commit Troops Once Peace Pact Is Signed, Ministers Say," *The Globe and Mail,* 18 February 1999.
306  Eggleton, w21 interview.
307  Baril, w21 interview.
308  Sallot and Freeman, "Chretien Offers Peacekeepers for Kosovo," *The Globe and Mail,* 30 January 1999; MacCharles, "Eggleton May Skip Troop Debate – Soldiers Would Go to Kosovo as Part of NATO-led Force," *Toronto Star,* 16 February 1999.
309  Martin and Fortmann, "Public Opinion and Canadian Internationalism after the Cold War."
310  Thompson, "Canada Could Send 800 Troops to Kosovo," *Toronto Star,* 18 February 1999.
311  Sallot and Freeman, "Chrétien Offers Peacekeepers for Kosovo."

312  Fowler, W21 interview. See also Hume, "Nazifying the Serbs, from Bosnia to Kosovo," in Hammond and Herman, eds., *Degraded Capability*, 70–8.

313  Martin, W21 interview.

314  Martin and Fortmann, "Public Opinion and Canadian Internationalism after the Cold War," 29.

315  Heinbecker, W21 interview.

316  Eggleton, W21 interview.

317  Axworthy, *Navigating a New World*, 185.

318  Fowler, W21 interview.

319  Eggleton, W21 interview.

320  Gee and Fraser, "Defiant Serbs Refuse to Back Down," *The Globe and Mail*, 27 March 1999.

321  Ibid.

322  Speirs, "Keeping Quiet about Kosovo," *Toronto Star*, 20 April 1999.

323  Ibid.

324  Quinn, "Local Serbs Pray for Their Families," *Toronto Star*, 29 March 1999; Collenette, W21 interview.

325  Lloyd Axworthy, W21 interview, Winnipeg MB, 21 July 2008.

326  Gee and Fraser, "Defiant Serbs Refuse to Back Down."

327  Watson, W21 interview.

328  Mark Fried, W21 interview, Ottawa, ON, 20 November 2008.

329  Boesveld, "Jean expresses sorrow over Canada's lack of action during Rwandan genocide," *The Globe and Mail*, 21 April 2010.

330  Baril, W21 interview.

331  Marleau quoted in Münster, "Access Czar Says Information Control 'Alarming' in Government," *The Hill Times*, 2 February 2009.

# Bibliography

Ackerman, Seth and Jim Naureckas. "Following Washington's Script: The United States Media and Kosovo." In Hammond and Herman, *Degraded Capability*, 97–110

Adelman, Howard and Astri Suhrke, eds. *The Path of a Genocide: The Rwanda Crisis from Uganda to Zaire*. New Brunswick, NJ: Transaction 1999

Adelman, Howard. "Canadian Policy in Rwanda." In Adelman and Suhrke, eds., *The Path of a Genocide*, 185–209

Axworthy, Lloyd. *Navigating a New World: Canada's Global Future*. Toronto: Alfred A. Knopf Canada 2003

Barnett, Michael N. *Eyewitness to a Genocide: The United Nations and Rwanda*. Ithaca: Cornell University Press 2002

Bartleman, James. *Rollercoaster: My Hectic Years as Jean Chrétien's Diplomatic Advisor, 1994–1998*. Toronto: McClelland and Stewart 2005

Bennet, Douglas J. "Confidential State Department Briefing Memorandum." 13 April 1994. Sent to Warren Christopher. Declassified 8 April 2003. National Security Archive, George Washington University. http://www.gwu.edu/~nsarchiv/NSAEBB/NSAEBB117/ Rw16.pdf (accessed 10 January 2009)

Bennet, Douglas J., George C. Moose, Conrad K. Harper and John Shattuck. "Secret State Department Action Memorandum, Has Genocide Occurred in Rwanda?" 5 May 1994. Sent to Secretary of the State Department. Declassified. National Security Archive,

George Washington University. http://www.gwu.edu/~nsarchiv/
NSAEBB/NSAEBB53/rwo52194.pdf (accessed 13 January 2009)

Berdal, Mats and Spyros Economides, eds. *United Nations Interventionism: 1991–2004*. Cambridge: Cambridge University Press 1996

Boesveld, Sarah. "Jean expresses sorrow over Canada's lack of action
during Rwandan genocide." *The Globe and Mail*, 21 April 2010

Brown, Ian. "A Presidential Showdown: Leno versus Letterman." *The
Globe and Mail*, 30 May 2009

Buckley, William Joseph, ed. *Kosovo: Contending Voices on Balkan
Interventions*. Grand Rapids: William B. Eerdmans Publishing Co.
2000

Canada. House of Commons Debates, Official Report (Hansard). Oral
Question Period. 5 May 1994. http://www2.parl.gc.ca/HousePubli-
cations/Publication.aspx?Language=E&Mode=1&Parl=35&Ses=1&
DocId=2332319 (accessed 28 May 2009)

Canada. House of Commons Debates, Official Report (Hansard). Oral
Question Period. 10 May 1994.http://www2.parl.gc.ca/HousePubli-
cations/Publication.aspx?Language=E&Mode=1&Parl1=35&Ses=1
&DocId=2332322&File=0 (accessed 28 May 2009)

Canadian Press. "Canada to Commit Troops Once Peace Pact Is
Signed, Ministers Say." *The Globe and Mail*, 18 February 1999

Castonguay, Jacques. *Les Casques bleus au Rwanda*. Paris: Éditions
L'Harmattan 1998

Clarke, Richard A. *Your Government Failed You: Breaking the Cycle
of National Security Disasters*. New York: Harper Collins 2008

Cohen, Andrew. *While Canada Slept: How We Lost Our Place in the
World*. Toronto: McClelland and Stewart 2003

Cohen, Jared. *One Hundred Days of Silence: America and the Rwanda
Genocide*. Lanham: Rowman and Littlefield 2007

Copson, Raymond W. *The Congressional Black Caucus and Foreign
Policy*. New York: Novinka Books 2003

Dallaire, Roméo. *Shake Hands with the Devil: The Failure of Humanity in Rwanda*. New York: Carroll & Graf Publishers 2003

Department of Foreign Affairs and International Trade. *Freedom from
Fear: Canada's Foreign Policy for Human Security*. Ottawa 1999

Des Forges, Alison. "Call to Genocide: Radio in Rwanda 1994." In
Thompson, ed., *The Media and the Rwanda Genocide*, 41–54

– *Leave None to Tell the Story*. New York and Paris: Human Rights
    Watch & International Federation of Human Rights 1999

Dykstra, J.M. "Rwanda: Tracing the Roots of Genocide." *Peace Maga-
    zine* 16, no. 6 (November-December 1997). http://archive.
    peacemagazine.org/v13n6p24.htm (accessed 20 February 2009)

Economides, Spyros. "Kosovo." In Mats Berdal and Spyros Econ-
    omides, eds., *United Nations Interventionism: 1991–2004*, 217–45.
    Cambridge: Cambridge University Press 1996

Egan, Patrick T. "The Kosovo Intervention and Collective Self
    Defence." *International Peacekeeping* 8, no. 3 (Autumn 2001):
    39–58

Executive Secretariat of the Operations Center at the US State Depart-
    ment. "Confidential Situation Report No.6." 8 April 1994. Sent
    to all state bureaus and offices. Declassified 27 November 1996.
    National Security Archive, George Washington University. http://
    www.gwu.edu/~nsarchiv/NSAEBB/NSAEBB119/Rw13.pdf (accessed 6
    January 2009)

Fowler, Robert. Memorandum to the Minister of National Defence
    David Collenette. 6 June 1994

Gee, Marcus and Graham Fraser. "Defiant Serbs Refuse to Back
    Down; the Debate: Who Gave Canadians 'a Licence to Kill'?" *The
    Globe and Mail*, 27 March 1999

Gendron, Robin S. *Towards a Francophone Community: Canada's
    Relations with France and French Africa, 1945–1968*. Montreal and
    Kingston: McGill-Queen's University Press 2006

Haglund, David and Allen Sens. "Kosovo and the Case of the (Not
    So) Free Riders: Portugal, Belgium, Canada and Spain." In Albrecht
    Schnabel and Ramesh Thakur, eds., *Kosovo and the Challenge of
    Humanitarian Intervention*, 181–201. Tokyo: United Nations Uni-
    versity Press 2000

Halperin, Morton H. "Winning the Peace: America's Goals in Kosovo."
    In Buckley, ed., *Kosovo*, 224–31

Hammond, Philip and Edward S. Herman, eds. *Degraded Capability:
    The Media and the Kosovo Crisis*. London: Pluto Press 2000

Herman, Edward S. and David Peterson. "CNN: Selling NATO's War
    Globally." In Hammond and Herman, eds., *Degraded Capability*,
    111–22

Hilsum, Lindsey. "Reporting Rwanda: The Media and Aid Agencies."
    In Thompson, ed., *The Media and the Rwanda Genocide*, 167–88
Hume, Mick. "Nazifying the Serbs, from Bosnia to Kosovo." In Ham-
    mond and Herman, eds., *Degraded Capability*, 70–8
Independent International Commission on Kosovo. *The Kosovo
    Report: Conflict, International Response, Lessons Learned*. New
    York: Oxford University Press 2000
International Centre for Human Rights and Democratic Development.
    "The Government and Armed Forces Responsible for the Reign of
    Terror in Rwanda." Press release, 8 March 1993. http://www.ddrd.
    ca/site/media/index.php?id=554&subsection=news (accessed 28
    May 2009)
Johnstone, Diana. "NATO and the New World Order: Ideals and Self-
    Interest." In Hammond and Herman, eds., *Degraded Capability*, 7–18
Jones, Bruce. "Rwanda." In Mats Berdal and Spyros Economides, eds.,
    *United Nations Interventionism: 1991–2004*, 139–67
Kiernan, Ben. *Blood and Soil: A World History of Genocide and Exter-
    mination from Sparta to Darfur*. New Haven and London: Yale
    University Press 2007
Kimonyo, Jean-Paul. "Rwanda: Ottawa est prié de s'impliquer à fond
    dans la lutte aux 'criminels de Kigali.'" *La Presse*, 19 April 1994
Kuperman, Alan J. "How the Media Missed the Rwanda Genocide." In
    Thompson, ed., *The Media and the Rwanda Genocide*, 256–61
Livingston, Stephen and Todd Eachus. "Rwanda: U.S. Policy and
    Television Coverage." In Adelman and Suhrke, eds., *The Path of a
    Genocide*, 209–31
Luttwack, Edward N. "Give War a Chance." In Buckley, ed., *Kosovo*,
    349–55
MacCharles, Tonda. "Eggleton May Skip Troop Debate – Soldiers
    Would Go to Kosovo as Part of NATO-led Force." *Toronto Star*, 16
    February 1999
Martin, Pierre and Michel Fortmann. "Public Opinion and Canadian
    Internationalism after the Cold War: Obstacle, Partner, or Scape-
    goat?" Presented at The Institute for Research on Public Policy Con-
    ference "Challenges to Governance: Military Interventions Abroad
    and Consensus at Home," Montreal, 17–18 November 2000. http://
    mistral.ere.umontreal.ca/~martinp/TextesPDF.htm (accessed 29
    April 2009)

Melvern, Linda. *A People Betrayed: The Role of the West in Rwanda's Genocide*. London and New York: Zed Books 2000

– *Conspiracy to Murder: The Rwandan Genocide*. London and New York: Verso 2004

– "Missing the Story: The Media and the Rwanda Genocide." In Thompson, ed., *The Media and the Rwanda Genocide*, 198–210

Mennecke, Martin. "Genocide in Kosovo?" In Samuel Totten and William S. Parsons, eds., *Century of Genocide: Critical Essays and Eyewitness Accounts*, 2nd ed., 449–54. New York: Routledge 2009

Mennecke, Martin, and Eric Markusen. "Genocide in Bosnia and Herzegovina." In Samuel Totten and William S. Parsons, eds., *Century of Genocide: Critical Essays and Eyewitness Accounts*, 2nd ed., 415–48. New York: Routledge 2009

Münster, Cynthia. "Access Czar Says Information Control 'Alarming' in Government." *The Hill Times*, 2 February 2009

Nazi, Fron. "Balkan Diaspora 1: The Albanian-American Community." In Buckley, ed., *Kosovo*, 149–52

Otunnu, Ogenga. "Rwandan Refugees and Immigrants in Uganda." In Adelman and Suhrke, eds., *The Path of a Genocide*, 3–29

PBS. PBS *Frontline Interview, "Ghosts of Rwanda," with US National Security Advisor Anthony Lake*. 15 December 2003. http://www.pbs.org/wgbh/pages/frontline/shows/ ghosts/interviews/lake.html (accessed 15 November 2008)

PBS. PBS *Frontline Interview, "Ghosts of Rwanda," with US Ambassador to the* UN *Madeleine Albright*. 25 February 2004. http://www.pbs.org/wgbh/pages/frontline/shows/ghosts/interviews/albright.html (accessed 18 November 2008)

PBS. PBS *Frontline Interview, "Ghosts of Rwanda," with US Assistant Secretary of State for African Affairs George Moose*. 21 November 2003. http://www.pbs.org/wgbh/pages/ frontline/shows/ghosts/interviews/moose.html (accessed 21 November 2008)

PBS. PBS *Frontline Interview, "Ghosts of Rwanda," with US Ambassador David P. Rawson*. 5 October 2003. http://www.pbs.org/wgbh/pages/frontline/shows/ghosts/interviews/rawson.html (accessed 12 November 2008)

PBS. PBS *Frontline Interview, "The Triumph of Evil," with US Deputy Assistant Secretary for African Affairs James Woods*. January 1999.

http://www.pbs.org/wgbh/pages/frontline/shows/evil/interviews/
woods.html (accessed 12 January 2009)

PBS. PBS *Frontline Interview, "The Triumph of Evil," with US State
Department Political Military Advisor Tony Marley.* January 1999.
http://www.pbs.org/wgbh/pages/frontline/shows/evil/interviews/
marley.html (accessed 12 January 2009)

Power, Samantha. *A Problem from Hell: America and the Age of
Genocide.* New York: Harper Perennial 2003

Quinn, Jennifer. "'Local Serbs Pray for Their Families – I'm Crying for
My People,' Tearful Woman Says." *Toronto Star,* 29 March 1999

Sallott, Jeff and Alan Freeman. "Chrétien Offers Peacekeepers for Kosovo." *The Globe and Mail,* 30 January 1999

Schabas, William A. *Genocide in International Law.* Cambridge: Cambridge University Press 2000

Shattuck, John. *Freedom on Fire: Human Rights Wars and America's
Response.* Cambridge: Harvard University Press 2003

Speirs, Rosemary. "Keeping Quiet about Kosovo." *Toronto Star,* 20
April 1999

Thompson, Allan. "Africans Best for Mediation, Ouellet says." *Toronto
Star,* 3 May 1994

– "Canada Could Send 800 Troops to Kosovo; Peacekeeping Mission
Debated in Commons." *Toronto Star,* 18 February 1999

Thompson, Allan, ed. *The Media and the Rwanda Genocide.* London: Pluto Press; Fountain Publishers; International Development
Research Centre 2007

United Nations. *United Nations Security Council Resolution 912
(1994).* 21 April 1994. United Nations. http://daccessdds.un.org/
doc/UNDOC/GEN/N94/190/85/PDF/N9419085.pdf?OpenElement
(accessed 28 May 2009)

United Nations. *United Nations Security Council Resolution 1199
(1998).* 23 September 1998. United Nations Interim Administration
Mission in Kosovo. http://www.un.org/peace/kosovo/98sc1199.htm
(accessed 10 January 2009)

United States Central Intelligence Agency. "National Intelligence
Daily." 8 April 1994. National Security Archive, George Washington
University. http://www.gwu.edu/~nsarchiv/NSAEBB/NSAEBB119/
Rw10.pdf (accessed 6 January 2009)

United States Defense Intelligence Agency. "Secret Defense Intelligence Report, *Rwanda: The Rwandan Patriotic Front's Offensive*," 9 May 1994. National Security Archive, George Washington University. http://www.gwu.edu/~nsarchiv/NSAEBB/NSAEBB53/rw050994.pdf (accessed 20 January 2009)

United States Department of State. "Report on the Visit of Ambassador Scheffer to the Border between the Former Republic of Macedonia and Kosovo, April 1–2 and Refugee Accounts of Atrocities." 7 April 1999. US State Department. http://www.state.gov/www/regions/eur/990407_scheffer_kosovo.html (accessed 10 February 2009)

United States Embassy, Ottawa. "Cable to U.S. State Department, *The Rwanda Crisis and Canada*." 13 May 1994. Sent to US Secretary of State. Declassified 24 July 2002. National Security Archive, George Washington University. http://www.gwu.edu/~nsarchiv/NSAEBB/NSAEBB117/Rw10.pdf (accessed 10 February 2009)

United States Secretary of State. "Confidential State Memorandum, *Working Group Formation to Deal with the Situation in Kigali and Bujumbura*." 8 April 1994. Sent to all Diplomatic and Consular Posts Immediate. Declassified 28 April 2000. National Security Archive, George Washington University. http://www.gwu.edu/~nsarchiv/NSAEBB/NSAEBB119/Rw8.pdf (accessed 15 January 2009)

United States Secretary of State. "Confidential State Department Action Memorandum." 15 April 1994. Sent to US Mission USUN New York. Declassified 4 May 2000. National Security Archive, George Washington University. http://www.gwu.edu/~nsarchiv/NSAEBB/NSAEBB53/rw041594.pdf (accessed 13 January 2009)

United States Undersecretary of Defense. "Confidential Memorandum, *Rwanda: Jamming Civilian Radio Broadcasts*." 5 May 1994. Sent to the Deputy Assistant to the President for National Security Affairs, National Security Council. Declassified 27 March 1995. National Security Archive, George Washington University. http://www.gwu.edu/~nsarchiv/NSAEBB/NSAEBB53/rw050594.pdf (accessed 20 January 2009)

Uvin, Peter. *Aiding Violence: The Development Enterprise in Rwanda*. West Hartford, Connecticut: Kumarian Press 1998

Vucinich, Nick. "Balkan Diaspora II: The History and Future of the Serbian Community in America." In Buckley, ed., *Kosovo*, 153–8

Walzer, Michael. "Kosovo." In Buckley, ed., *Kosovo*, 333–5

Winter, Roger. "Power, Not Tribalism, Stokes Rwanda's Slaughter." *The Globe and Mail*, 14 April 1994

Wright, David. "Kosovo: Inside the North Atlantic Council." In David Haglund, ed., *New NATO, New Century: Canada, the United States, and the Future of the Atlantic Alliance*. Kingston: Queen's University Centre for International Relations and Canadian Institute of Strategic Studies 2000

# The Montreal Institute For Genocide and Human Rights Studies: An Overview

The Montreal Institute for Genocide and Human Rights Studies (MIGS) was founded in 1986, based in the departments of History and Sociology/Anthropology at Concordia University. The main missions of MIGS are to develop and manage major research programs focused on the prevention and prosecution of genocide and crimes against humanity, to educate comparatively about genocide, and to help survivors and their children end their isolation by building bridges with other survivors of genocide and mass atrocity crimes.

Drawing on its research, MIGS furthers understanding of the history, sociology, and international legal frameworks pertaining to genocide, crimes against humanity, and attempts at reconciliation in their wake. To advance these goals, MIGS organizes workshops and conferences, sponsors lectures, issues reports, prepares books and articles, and trains students specializing in genocide studies at the undergraduate and graduate levels. MIGS works locally, nationally, and internationally to educate members of the public, the media, and government.

MIGS is recognized around the world as Canada's pre-eminent centre for the study of genocide. In partnership with Gen. Roméo Dallaire, its distinguished Senior Fellow, MIGS launched the Will to Intervene (W2I) Project in September 2007. W2I is designed to develop practical tools to operationalize the principles of

the Canadian-sponsored report on the responsibility to protect, which aims to prevent future Cambodias and Rwandas.
The MIGS project focuses attention on the critical gap in our
understanding of how to mobilize the domestic political will to
intervene. MIGS and Roméo Dallaire seek to bridge that gap with
this major study based on interviews with key US and Canadian
political leaders at the very highest levels about their decisions
over intervention in Rwanda and Kosovo. Drawing on these
interviews, MIGS is making practical recommendations to NGO
directors, media executives, political leaders, and others, helping
them to promote effective measures intended to prevent future
genocides.

MIGS faculty and graduate students are important participants
in "Life Stories of Montrealers Displaced by War, Genocide and
Other Human Rights Violations," a major research project based
at Concordia. Life Stories CURA combines the talents and ener-
gies of thirty-nine academics and nineteen Montreal community
organizations. MIGS brings its expertise to "Comparative Perspectives on Montreal Survivors of Atrocity Crimes," which will
interview 300 Montrealers who survived mass atrocities, including the Holocaust, Cambodia, and Rwanda. The oral histories
of these survivors and their descendants, collected by the Comparative Perspectives team, are contributing to the production
of school curriculum materials, programs for television, radio,
film, theatre, museum exhibits, and cultural center programs.
"Life Stories" is supported with funds from the Social Science
and Humanities Research Council of Canada and Concordia
University.

In recent years, Concordia faculty members and graduate students from Communications, English, Geography, Humanities,
and Political Science have joined in the work of MIGS, as have
colleagues from other universities. MIGS collaborates closely
with the Canada Research Chair in Public History, the Centre
for Oral History and Digital Storytelling, and the Centre for
Ethnographic Research in the Aftermath of Violence based in the
Concordia History Department. Through its work with graduate
and undergraduate students, MIGS has trained the largest group
of genocide specialists in Canada.

## SUPPORT FOR MIGS

MIGS is an official research centre of the Faculty of Arts and Science of Concordia University. Monetary contributions to advance its research projects, publications, conferences, and multimedia projects are welcome and will be prominently recognized. They should be mailed to:

Advancement (re. MIGS)
Concordia University
Faculty of Arts & Science
1455 de Maisonneuve Blvd. West
Montreal, QC
Canada H3G 1M8